Prestel Museum Guide

Städelsches Kunstinstitut and Städtische Galerie Frankfurt/M.

Prestel

Munich · London · New York

Edited by Bodo Brinkmann

Contributors:
Bodo Brinkmann   BB
Ingrid Ehrhardt   IE
Ursula Grzechca-Mohr   GM
Michael Maek-Gérard   MG
Jochen Sander   JS
Sabine Schulze   SS
Hans-Joachim Ziemke   HJZ

Works marked SM-V are the property of the
Friends of the Städel Museum (Städelscher Museums-Verein)

Contents

The Building and the Collection

The Städel is an open museum, rich in tradition and at the same time modern, with a special atmosphere and flair. Its collection ranges from masterpieces of the early 14th century to late Gothic art, from the Re-naissance and Baroque periods to the age of Goethe, and from the 19th century to the present, placing it among the foremost international collections. The presentation of each individual work complements and heightens its aesthetic effect within a dynamic spatial relationship, effortlessly revealing its beauty to the observer.

The actual appearance of the building is strongly influenced by the alterations it underwent between 1997 and 1999 and by the expansion of the museum in order to ensure broader public appeal. In turn, it has been the public, particularly the citizens of Frankfurt and the Rhine-Main area, who have made the renovations and additions to the Städel Art Institute possible over the years, maintaining the spirit of the Frankfurt banker and merchant Johann Friedrich Städel who founded the museum in 1815.

The superb location on the banks of the River Main sets the museum apart. Its Neo-Renaissance facade, completed in the 1870s, is impressive, not least because of its sculptural features. Despite the heaviness of the projecting pavilions at both ends of the Main Building which were badly damaged during World War II and rebuilt in the 1960s, the museum is characterized by a sense of lightness. The optical reduction of massive walls to apparently thin surfaces was an architectural convention of the era in which the Städel was rebuilt. Frankfurt architect Johannes Krahn developed this principle, which also

dominates the interior of the building. It remains compellingly effective and is carried through to the last detail. Bronze ornamentation, made from the designs of sculptor Hans Mettel, reinforces the effect.

The recently completed alterations to the building were carried out in compliance with this principle of architectural lightness, resulting in rooms that seem suspended in space. Jochem Jourdan, the architect in charge of the renovation, preserved the clarity of the postwar architectural style. He merely diminished the contradiction between the modern interior and the historic exterior of the building and replaced the compartmentalized small rooms that had formerly followed one another with the clarity of larger spaces arranged along an extended axis. This provides the advantage of better exhibition space for the collec-

tion. The best example of this is the entrance foyer, whose imposing verticality is, on the one hand, reinforced by opening the view upwards into the central dome. On the other hand, the floor mosaic by New York artist Valerie Jaudon creates the illusion of depth through the use of perspective.

The emphasis on the axial symmetry of the construction is advantageous to the new arrangement of the collection. The 20th century occupies the central section. Its Garden Wing makes a 90 degree turn and encloses the collection of painting and sculpture, which proceeds in reverse chronological order back to the year 1800. The works of Old Masters are divided amongst the east and west sections of the Main Wing. The two centuries preceding the Reformation are to the east, and the centuries following it, encom-

passing the period up to the turn of the 18th century into the 19th, are to the west. Within this chronological order the collection is arranged geographically—although the spatial intersection offers exciting opportunities for comparison.

This intentional, concentrated presentation of the paintings is reflected in the color used in the rooms. Gray tones alternate with intense color, turning the gallery into a walk-through sculpture and creating a unified space in which the art can be thoroughly experienced.

For the past 2,500 years philosophical thought has supported the notion that art is man's highest

achievement. Collecting art, preserving it, studying it, as well as creating a broad awareness and interest in art is the museum's main objective. For this reason, the museum has updated its methods from generation to generation, especially in cases when one epoch gives way to another. One of the Städel's aims has been to maintain and expand its role as a focal urban center for communication and personal fulfillment.

To achieve a balance between the unchanging collection of Old Masters and the variable presentation of works from the 19th and 20th centuries, along with temporary special exhibitions, the space allotted to the Collection of Prints and Drawings has been aesthetically and technically modernized. It is now possible to present the museum's own works on paper, which for reasons of conservation had been kept in specially darkened strong rooms, in more frequently changing exhibitions, enhanced from time to time by loans from other collections. The building on Holbein Street, designed by Gustav Peichl and completed in 1990, is the venue for temporary exhibitions featuring specific themes, the works of selected artists, or art historically important periods.

In addition to his art collection and a large sum of money, Johann Friedrich Städel endowed the museum with an extensive collection of books, which has become the basis of the Städel's art library. Open to the public as a reference library, it has gained in relevance and provides further information and access with its bookstore and museum shop.

The collection of paintings, however, remains the heart of the Städel. A semi-public space has developed peripherally—the new café restaurant has brought the urbanity of the city and the region to the museum, providing the visitor with a place of

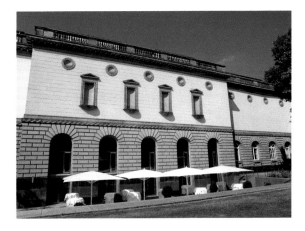

tranquillity, enjoyment, conversation, and reflection. The café restaurant also has an entrance on Holbein Street, and its transparent architecture of glass and steel attracts guests and remains open long after the museum has closed. The festive atmosphere spreads from there in widening circles to adjacent areas. The old foyer adjoins the restaurant and leads to the garden room, whose high windows provide a view of the garden with a panorama that changes with the seasons. In the summer the terrace sets the stage for the garden's lush greenery.

Museums provide a link between art and the public. The Städel wants visitors to approach the essence of art and experience the dynamic sensual and intellectual adventure art has to offer.

History

1816 Death of Johann Friedrich Städel. His Testament is opened, revealing his wish that an art institute be founded in his name, with five administrators to be chosen from among Frankfurt's citizens. Städel bequeaths his house on Rossmarkt, the art collection it contains, and his fortune to the institute, which is to serve two purposes: to maintain a public art collection and to promote the education of new artists.

1817 Distant relatives challenge the will and tie up the estate in litigation that will drag on for 11 years and prevent the administration from continuing the work of the institute. Karl Friedrich Wendelstadt is made the museum's first "inspector."

1930 Philipp Veit, a painter of the Nazarene School, is appointed headmaster of the art school and director of the gallery. Stephan Lochner's *Martyrdom of the Apostles* (p. 28) is purchased for the collection.

1833 The institute moves into a building especially modified to house it, on Neue Mainzer Street. Veit's fresco cycle, *Christianity introducing the Arts in Germany*, decorates one hall.

1840 Johann David Passavant becomes inspector, having already served the institute in various capacities. His expertise results in a number of brilliant acquisitions,

among them Botticelli's *Ideal Portrait of a Young Woman* and three panels by the Master of Flémalle (pp. 18, 45). The same year, Friedrich Overbeck completes *The Triumph of Religion in the Arts* (p. 94), his pictorial representation of the philosophy of the Nazarene School, commissioned by the institute's administration in 1829.

1850 Passavant acquires additional works at the auction of the art collection of King William II of the Netherlands. These include the *Lucca Madonna* by Jan van Eyck (p. 47) and drawings by Raphael.

1861 Gerhard Malss becomes inspector and rearranges the gallery and the print collection.

1870 Important paintings, including Holbein's *Portrait of Simon George of Cornwall* (p. 37), are purchased at the Brentano-Birckenstock auction.

1878 The institute moves into its new building on Schaumainkai.

1885 Georg Kohlbacher becomes inspector.

1889 Henry Thode becomes director (the position formerly called "inspector"). He is interested in early Italian painting and acquires, among other works, Meo da Siena's altar panels (p. 14).

1891 Heinrich Weizsäcker appointed director. He compiles the first catalogue of the complete collection.

1899 Foundation of the Friends of the Städel Museum through the efforts of Leopold Sonnemann, publisher of the *Frankfurter Zeitung*.

1904 Ludwig Justi becomes director. He acquires the museum's first Monet as well as Rembrandt's great painting, *The Blinding of Samson* (p. 60).

1906 Georg Swarzenski, a lover of medieval and modern art, becomes director. One of his first acquisitions is Cranach's *Torgau Altar* (p. 41). By the outbreak of World War I Swarzenski has acquired works of virtually all of the French Impressionists that are in the current Städel collection. Afterwards, he collects the works of contemporary artists: Ernst Ludwig Kirchner and Franz Marc (pp. 126, 132), as well as works by Edward Munch and Oskar Kokoschka. Later, he adds paintings by Picasso and Braque but, above all, works by the Städel School instructor Max Beckmann. In order to expand the collection of modern art, the Städtische Galerie (Municipal Gallery) is founded.

1922 Swarzenski arranges an exchange of paintings between the Historisches Museum and the Städel. As a result, the Städel holds superb works of Early German painting on permanent loan, including the *Little Garden of Paradise*, the *Dominican Altar* and two panels by Grünewald from the *Heller Altar* (pp. 25, 33, 40)

1928 The Hohenzollern collection from Sigmaringen is exhibited in the Städel and subsequently sold. Swarzenski manages to acquire important Early German works from it for the museum, including *The Resurrection of Christ* by the Master of the Housebook, the portrait by Holbein the Elder and Altdorfer's *Adoration of the Magi* (pp. 31, 36, 43). In the same year Swarzenski is appointed general director of all Frankfurt museums.

1933 Swarzenski, a Jew, is relieved of all his municipal positions but remains director of the Städel until his retirement. In 1938 he emigrates to the United States.

1937 Condemned as "degenerate art" by the National Socialists, 77 paintings and more than 700 prints are confiscated. Among them are famous works such as Vincent van Gogh's *Portrait of Dr. Gachet*, which has been given to the Städel as a gift in 1912.

1938 Ernst Holzinger becomes director. In the same year he acquires the collection of Lulu Müller, with works by Victor Müller and other artists. One year later he obtains the Eiser-Küchler collection with works by Hans Thoma. Thereafter, the museum's collection is stored outside Frankfurt to prevent damage during World War II. Virtually nothing is lost despite the heavy damage to the building during air raids.

1950 Holzinger acquires the central panel of the *Tabernacle of the Exaltation of the True Cross* by Adam

Elsheimer (p. 80), the reassembly of which will take the next three decades. The remaining six panels are acquired in succession by the Städel. The Friends of the Städel Museum, which owns four of the panels, is instrumental in their acquisition.

1962   With the help of the Frankfurter Sparkasse, the museum succeeds in getting back the Matisse still life (p. 122) confiscated in 1937.

1963   The building is reconstructed based on plans by architect Johannes Krahn.

1972   A sensational collection drive raises funds to purchase Beckmann's *Synagogue in Frankfurt*.

1974   Klaus Gallwitz becomes director. His acquisitions include works of the classical modern period (Kirchner, Beckmann) and especially those by postwar artists (Karel Appel, Emil Schumacher) along with contemporary artists such as Georg Baselitz, Anselm Kiefer and Dan Flavin (pp. 140, 148, 150).

1982   Watteaus' *Pilgrimage to the Island of Cythera* marks yet another spectacular acquisition of an Old Master painting that enhances the collection of 18th-century French paintings. Some years earlier the museum obtained a still life by Chardin (pp. 75, 76).

1990   The Holbein Street extension, designed by Gustav Peichl, is completed. Part of the new wing is used to house the collection of 20th-century art; the other is used for special exhibitions.

1994   Herbert Beck becomes director and undertakes the renovation of the museum.

The Gallery

Italian Painting of the Middle Ages and the Renaissance

Deodato di Orlandi (active ca. 1300)
St. John in Mourning
Inv. No. 1887
Tempera and oil on poplar,
54 x 43 cm

What today appears to be an independent picture portraying the mournful evangelist John is in fact a mere fragment, the only existing portion of a monumental painted cross. It occupied an extension of the trunk portion of the cross upon which Christ is crucified. Square panels extended along the cross beam, with depictions of the mourning Virgin and St. John. Such painted crosses (similar to the high-relief triumphal crosses of the North) hung in the entrance arches of large churches, usually above the choir screen or the entrance to the chancel.   *JS*

Meo da Siena (died 1333/34)
Double-sided painted altar panel
showing Christ on the heavenly
throne, the 12 Apostles and the
Madonna enthroned with saints
Inv. Nos. 1201, 1202
Tempera and oil on poplar,
60 x 305 cm and 61 x 305 cm

The panel, painted by Meo da Siena, was not split into two halves until the 18th century. From the beginning of the 1330s it served as the
double-sided panel on the high altar of the Benedictine Abbey of San
Pietro in the Umbrian city of Peru-
gia. Hugolino, the donor and abbot,
is portrayed as the small kneeling
figure at the foot of the throne of
the Madonna and Christ Child.
While Christ on his throne is
flanked by the 12 Apostles, the Vir-

gin is shown surrounded by saints,
whose relics the monastery pos-
sessed and who were therefore
especially revered.   JS

Bartolomeo Bulgarini
(ca. 1300/10–1378)
The Blinding of St. Victor
Inv. No. 2135
Tempera and oil on poplar,
40 x 39 cm

The small painted panel shows the
gruesome martyrdom of St. Victor. It
was part of the predella of an altarpiece that was displayed along with
Duccio's *Maestà* and three other altarpieces in the cathedral in Siena.
The principal painting depicted the
Nativity and was dedicated to the
Virgin, the main patron saint of the

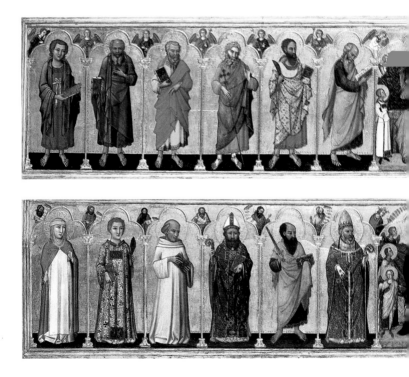

city of Siena. The predella scenes commemorated Victor, a popular saint in that region. Robert von Hirsch donated the panel to the Städel in memory of its director Georg Swarzenski. *JS*

Barnaba da Modena
(ca. 1328/30–after 1386)
Madonna and Child
Inv. No. 807
Tempera and oil on poplar,
118 x 86 cm

This Madonna panel, signed and dated 1367, is among the earliest works by Barnaba da Modena, who was primarily active in Genoa. It was originally the central panel of a large altarpiece. Where it originally stood and what happened to the remaining panels is unknown. Although the artist's use of green pigment under the flesh tones and rich gilding of the Virgin's robes clearly link him to the Italo-Byzantine icon tradition, his portrayal of the tender relationship between the Madonna and Child and his life-like representation of the latter clearly demonstrate that he was also familiar with the painting styles of Siena and Florence. *JS*

Fra Angelico (ca. 1395–1455)
Madonna and Child enthroned
surrounded by Angels
Inv. No. 838
Tempera and oil on poplar,
37 x 30 cm

This small panel was painted in the early 1420s by the Florentine monk and painter Fra Angelico. It shows the Madonna on a throne surrounded by 12 angels. Its small format, exquisite detail, and rich gilding indicate that it probably served the unknown patron who commissioned it as a private devotional object as well as proof of his cultivated artistic taste. *JS*

Andrea Mantegna (1431–1509)
St. Mark the Evangelist
Inv. No. 1046
Tempera and oil on canvas,
81 x 64 cm

This painting, now in Frankfurt, is among the earliest known works of the great Renaissance artist Andrea Mantegna. The work, painted ca. 1450, is a fine example of Mantegna's ability to combine his knowledge of the principles of perspec-

tive along with his confident rendering of various materials and reflecting surfaces in the manner of the Early Netherlandish painters. In this he far exceeded anything his contemporaries were able to achieve with tempera. *JS*

Sandro Botticelli (1445–1510)
Ideal Portrait of a Woman
Inv. No. 936
Tempera and oil on poplar,
82 x 54 cm

Similar to Bartolomeo Veneto's *Ideal Portrait of a Woman*, Botticelli's larger-than-life profile study, painted in 1480, is not a portrait in the strict sense of the word. Rather, as the fantastical outfit indicates, it is an idealized portrayal of a nymph in mythological clothing. The young woman resembles Simonetta Vespucci, Giuliano de'Medici's mistress. The medallion on her necklace, an ancient cameo from the Medici collection, also places her in the inner circle of the Florentine banking family. The large portrait was originally intended as part of a cycle of paintings, which was most probably added to the wood paneling of a palazzo in Florence. *JS*

Bartolomeo Veneto
(active 1500–1530)
Ideal Portrait of a Woman
Inv. No. 1077
Tempera and oil on poplar,
44 x 34 cm

The painting, long believed to be a portrait of Lucrezia Borgia, the scandalous daughter of a pope, is in fact the portrait of an unknown lady who had herself painted as Flora, the Goddess of Spring. Her fantastic costume with its turban, wig, and exposed breast, as well as the sprig of flowers in her right hand, indicate her role.   *JS*

Carlo Crivelli
(ca. 1430/35–ca. 1495)
The Angel Gabriel and the Annunciation
Inv. No. 841, 841A
Tempera and oil on poplar,
61 x 45 cm

These two perfectly preserved panels depict the Annunciation with loving detail. Originally they were part of a large, multipaneled altarpiece that also contained the Salvator Mundi (now in collection of the Abegg Foundation in Riggisberg). The work was created by the Venetian painter Carlo Crivelli in 1482 for

the Dominican church or cathedral of Camerino in Le Marche in central Italy. By the early 19th century the altarpiece had been dismantled. Its main panels showed the enthroned Madonna and Child, SS. Peter and Dominic, and the martyrdom of SS. Peter and Venantius. Depictions of other saints decorated the predella. These parts of the altarpiece are now in the Brera Art Gallery in Milan. JS

Giovanni Bellini
(ca. 1430/35–1516)
(and Bellini workshop)
Madonna and Child with SS. John and Elisabeth
Inv. Nr. 853
Tempera and oil on poplar,
72 x 90 cm

This painting was executed at the beginning of the 16th century in the studio of the Venetian painter Giovanni Bellini. It depicts the half-length figures of the Madonna holding the Christ Child, John the Baptist as well as an elder female saint, probably Elisabeth, John's mother. They are shown behind a balustrade, against a blue sky. This *sacra conversazione* is one of a number of closely related works based on Bellini's painting of the figures in full. These were reproduced in Bellini's workshop, using standardized patterns for the figures and depicting the saints according to the wishes of the respective customer commissioning the work. Trade convention dictated that the artist signed these paintings, although he may have been only minimally involved in their execution. JS

Pietro Vannucci, known as Perugino
(after 1450–1523)
Madonna and Child with St. John
Inv. No. 843
Tempera and oil on poplar,
68 x 51 cm

Giovanni Battista di Jacopo, known as Rosso Fiorentino
(1494–1540)
Madonna and Child with St. John
Inv. No. 952
Tempera and oil on poplar,
105 x 82 cm

Perugino painted this work toward the end of the 1490s. It shows the Madonna holding the Christ Child, and St. John the Baptist as an infant worshipping him.   *JS*

This 1515 painting of the Madonna, Christ Child and young St. John, is one of the largest panels by the great Florentine Mannerist known as Rosso Fiorentino. His *maniera*, or special style, is apparent in the attractive painting technique he used and in his relaxed composition, the preliminary sketching of which was deliberately left visible. Its most striking aspect, however, is the use of antique pagan models in the portrayal of Christian saints—a feature

that shocked many of the artists's contemporaries. The Madonna, in a tight robe revealing the contours of her body, evokes Venus, while the two children resemble Amor and a youthful Bacchus. *JS*

Peter de Kempeneer (1503–1580)
Portrait of a Lady
Inv. No. 946
Tempera and oil on poplar,
114 x 79 cm

The combination of an Italian style of portraiture along with a Netherlandish approach to landscape resulted in decades of controversy over the true identity of the painter of this portrait of an unknown lady. Its recent attribution to the Netherlandish painter Peter de Kempeneer is especially convincing because it addresses the contradictional hints to the picture's location and style. De Kempeneer was trained in a Brussels workshop and traveled to Italy as a young man, where he worked for Italian patrons in Emilia-Romagna. This painting apparently was produced during this period. Several years later de Kempeneer went to Spain and, under the name of Pedro Campaña, became one of the leading 16th-century artists active on the Iberian Peninsula. *JS*

Jacopo Carucci, known as Pontormo
(1494–1557)
Portrait of a Lady
Inv. No. 1136
Tempera and oil on poplar,
90 x 71 cm

This portrait of an unidentified lady dressed in red is among the most important works of the Italian Mannerist school of painting. Pontormo, who is believed to have painted this portrait with the help of his student and colleague Agnolo Bronzino, expressed the self-confidence and social standing of the young woman, who was probably a member of one of Florence's leading families, by using a most daring composition. The observer is kept at a respectful distance from the figure by the arm of the chair, which is drawn parallel to the picture plane, despite the frontal pose of the sitter. The depiction of light and shadow upon the niche behind the woman is both sophisticated and simple at the same time, and contributes enormously to the painting's impact. The brightest side of her face is presented against the deepest shadow of the niche, while the shaded side is painted against the lightest surface. *JS*

**Alessandro Bonvicino,
known as Moretto da Brescia**
(ca. 1490–1554)
Madonna and Child enthroned with
the Four Latin Church Fathers
Inv. No. 916
Oil on canvas, 284 x 87 cm

Moretto's *sacra conversazione* with the
Madonna and Christ Child surrounded by the Fathers of the Church is one
of the few large Renaissance altarpieces in the Frankfurt collection. Although this painting, which was completed in the 1540s, could only have
stood upon an altar dedicated to the
Church Fathers (because of their se-
lection instead of other, more common, saints), it has not been possible
to determine where the work was
originally displayed or the identity of
the patron who commissioned it. *JS*

Early German Painting

Master of the Garden of Paradise
(active ca. 1400/20)
Little Garden of Paradise
Inv. No. HM 54 (on loan
from the Historisches Museum)
Tempera and oil on oak,
26 x 33 cm

This is the most famous Early German painting in the Städel collection. It combines the realistic observation of nature with the courtly charm of the "International Gothic" style popular around 1400. The garden presents 24 different kinds of plants and 12 species of birds. Its central theme, however, is laid out in a consciously enigmatic manner. The Virgin is the central figure in this garden, which is identifiable as the Garden of Eden by the presence of the Tree of Life and the Tree of Knowledge. She is surrounded by saints, whose attributes are so subtly incorporated into the composition that they are difficult to recognize at first glance. Closer examination reveals that the female figures on the left are probably Dorothee, Barbara, and Catharine. The male figures on the right are the Archangel Michael, and SS. George and Oswald. They are not ranked according to celestial hierarchy but appear instead in an apparently casual social setting, although segregated by gender, as required by the church at the time. The iconography probably followed the wishes of the patron who commissioned the work for his private devotion.   *BB*

Middle Rhenish Master
(active ca. 1330/50)
Altenberg Altar
Left wing:
The Annunciation,
The Visitation,
The Nativity,
The Adoration of the Magi.
Right wing:
St. Michael,
The Coronation of the Virgin,
St. Elizabeth,
The Death of the Virgin
Inv. No. SG 358-361

Tempera and oil on fir,
each wing 154 x 119 cm

The two wings of the altarpiece
from the Premonstratensian Abbey
Altenberg near Wetzlar were originally fixed to a shrine containing a
statue of the Madonna and Christ
Child. Today, the shrine is preserved
in Braunfels Castle and the statue is
in the Bavarian National Museum in
Munich. The panel in the lower right
corner of the left wing, showing the
Three Magi bringing offerings to the

Christ Child refers to this once central figure. The lower left panel on the right wing depicts St. Elisabeth of Hungary clothing a beggar in a precious ermine-lined cloak. Behind her is a nun, probably representing Elizabeth's daughter Gertrud, abbess at Altenberg, who was interred in the choir of the church and beatified in 1348. The two wings were hinged between the narrow and broad panels, which meant that it was possible to fold them. This unusual feature allowed three different views of the altarpiece: fully opened, fully closed, or folded inwards/outwards. The unusual construction signifies a period of experimentation in the early history of the reversible altarpiece. Perhaps this one stood on the high altar and was removed in the Baroque period to the nuns' gallery, where it was rediscovered in the 19th century and turned over to the Prince zu Solms-Braunfels. The Städel acquired the panels from him in 1925.

BB

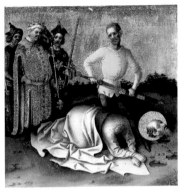

Stefan Lochner
(ca. 1410–1451)
Two wings of an altarpiece
depicting the Martyrdom
of the Apostles
Inv. Nos. 821-832
Tempera and oil on walnut,
123 x 81 cm each

Stefan Lochner is the most important 15th-century painter of the Cologne School. The Städel purchased
the two wings of Lochner's altarpiece showing the martyrdom of the
Apostles from Cologne collector To-
setti in 1830. The outer panels, depicting standing saints, are now in

the Alte Pinakothek in Munich. It is possible that both the Frankfurt and Munich panels originally flanked the famous painting of the Last Judgement in the Wallraf-Richartz Museum in Cologne. The altarpiece may originally have been painted for a chapel in the Church of the Holy Apostles in Cologne. The scenes of martyrdom exemplify Lochner's dramatic composition and his highly detailed realism. The artists did not refrain from depicting the most gruesome acts, as the horrible torture of St. Bartholomew aptly demonstrates.

BB

Master of the Covarrubias Madonna
(active ca. 1440)
Rest on the Flight into Egypt
Tempera and oil on spruce,
36 x 33 cm

This panel is part of an altarpiece probably painted by this German artist during his travels in Italy. The other panels are now in Liège, Venice, and Modena. The painting, with its impetuous composition, is the product of a vibrant imagination that shows all the miracles that could have possibly happened to the Holy Family on their flight into Egypt. It is characteristic of the radical changes that occurred when artists trained in the International Gothic style came under the influence of Netherlandish painting after 1400, inspiring German painters as well to move on to new forms of expression. Before traveling through Italy, this artist may even have spent some time working in the Bruges workshop of Jan van Eyck (see p. 47). *BB*

Master BM (active ca. 1500/10)
(successor of Martin Schongauer)
The Nativity
Inv. No. SG 444
Tempera and oil on oak,
38 x 30 cm

The artist, who is best known for his engravings, signed some of these with the initials BM. This small

panel relies heavily on Martin Schongauer's motifs without actually copying a work of the famous Alsatian master. The painting shows the Nativity in a snow-covered landscape. The icy ground on the left of the picture is tinted red by the winter sun, which is low on the horizon. Shepherds gather outside the stable, bending over its railing in adoration of the Christ Child. In the background, Joseph approaches along a path with Zelomi and Salome, the two midwives who, according to legend, came to the stable to assist the Virgin giving birth. *BB*

Master of the Housebook
(active 1470–1500)
The Resurrection of Christ
Inv. No. SG 447
Tempera and oil on fir,
132 x 77 cm

The Master of the Housebook was the leading exponent of the realistic Netherlandish style of painting in the middle Rhine area between 1450 and 1500. His powerful view of the Resurrection was the right panel of an altarpiece that once stood in Speyer cathedral. The central panel is now in the Augustiner Museum in Freiburg. *BB*

Wolfgang Beurer
(active 1485–1500)
(Master WB)
Portrait of a Man and a Woman
Inv. No. 334, 335
Tempera and oil on lime,
45 x 33 each

Master of the Pfullendorf Altar
(active ca. 1500)
The Nativity from the
Pfullendorf Altar
Inv. No. SG 455
Tempera and oil on fir,
103 x 71 cm

This early example of portraiture depicting a couple comes from the original collection of Johann Friedrich Städel. The two panels are precursors of the revolutionary double portrait by Conrad Faber (see p. 44). Beurer was, until recently, referred to as Master WB, the signature he used on some of his copperplate engravings. He appears to have worked in the same middle Rhine area as the Master of the Housebook did. Beurer also painted an altarpiece for the cathedral in Mainz, designed the stained glass windows for the church of the Holy Virgin in Hanau, and illuminated a prayer book for Worms. *BB*

This anonymous artist has been named after the altarpiece that probably originally stood in Pfullendorf.

The panels depicting the Annunciation, the Visitation, the Nativity, and the Death of the Virgin are in the Städel. The rest of the panels are in the Staatsgalerie in Stuttgart. The artist worked in the workshop of Bartholomew Zeitblom in Ulm and appears to have been influenced by Bernard Strigel from Memmingen.   *BB*

Hans Holbein the Elder
(ca. 1465–1524)
High Altar of the Dominican Church in Frankfurt, 1501

Exterior:
The Tree of Jesse and the Tree of the Dominican Order

Interior:
Christ Taken Prisoner, Christ before Pontius Pilate, The Flagellation, The Crowning with Thorns, Ecce Homo, The Crucifixion, The Resurrection
Predella:
The Entry into Jerusalem, The Cleansing of the Temple, The Last Supper, The Washing of the Feet, The Agony in the Garden
Inv. No. HM 6—20, LG 1
(on loan from the Historisches Museum and the Union of the Catholic Church Communities of Frankfurt)
Wood,
Each panel approx. 167 x 152 cm

When Frankfurt's Dominicans decided to renovate their collegiate church, they needed a new altarpiece and brought in Hans Holbein the Elder from Augsburg to paint it. He came with at least two assistants, his brother Sigismund and Leonhard Beck, and the three staid in the monastery for several years until the work was completed. They created the four wings of a double folding altarpiece, whose shrine probably contained carved wooden figures. Only two panels, one in Hamburg and one in Basle, remain from the Feast Day side of the altarpiece. The

predella, however, and the scenes from the Passion of Christ, on the first side of the folding screen, have survived almost completely intact. The clear, somewhat conventional composition and brilliant colors were meant to convey the story of the Passion of Christ to viewers from afar. In contrast, the outside of the altarpiece is far more unusual. Mirroring the Tree of Jesse on the left wing, the Dominican brothers had a "genealogical" tree of their order painted on the right. All important personages from the history of the order are represented: St. Dominic himself, Thomas Aquinas, Albertus Magnus, etc. Their features are so life-like and true to detail that the pictures appear to be individual portraits and may indeed have been modeled on monks living in the monastery under Prior Johann of Wilnau, whose name appears in the inscription in the center. Holbein's great talent for portraiture (see also below) was thus exploited by the extraordinarily self-confident Dominicans to promote the fame of their order.   *BB*

Hans Holbein the Elder
(ca. 1465–1524)
Portrait of a member of the Weiss Family from Augsburg, 1522
Inv. No. SG 457
Tempera and oil on lime,
42 x 35 cm

With his superb skills of observation, Holbein the Elder reveals the pretentiousness of this scion of a patrician Augsburg family. This apparently did not bother Holbein's patron, who commissioned the portrait as a painted proposal of mar-

riage. No less than three inscriptions on the hilt of his sword and his fashionable dog whistle proclaim his merits (among others, NOTH LEI[DE]T ER NIT = "He lacketh nought"). The proposal was apparently successful. A companion piece painted shortly afterwards, now in a private collection, depicts the wife of Mr. Weiss.   *BB*

Barthel Beham (1502–1540)
Portrait of Hans Urmiller
with his Son
Inv. No. 919
Tempera and oil on spruce,
65 x 47 cm

This artist, who was banned from his hometown for expressing his atheistic views, succeeded in obtaining a position at the Munich court of Duke Wilhelm IV of Bavaria, where he worked from 1527 on, primarily as a portraitist. Our picture has a counterpart, now in Philadelphia, which depicts Urmiller's wife with a daughter.   *BB*

Hans Holbein the Younger
(1497/98–1543)
Portrait of Simon George of Cornwall
Inv. No. 1065
Tempera and oil on oak,
ø 31 cm

As Henry VIII's court painter, Holbein the Younger probably met the British aristocrat from Cornwall at court in London. Although the details of the commission are unknown, the occasion for the picture may well have been amorous, perhaps similar to the Weiss portrait (see far left), meant as a proposal of marriage. Both the carnation and the small clip on the cap are indications of this. The clip depicts the ancient legend of Leda and the Swan, and thereby hints at the erotic intentions of the sitter, in a manner befitting his education and social status. Simon George obviously wanted to make a fashionable impression, so he had himself portrayed wearing a lavish costume reflecting the current trend. He also chose to have his portrait painted in the most modern format

of his time, a profile in the round, modeled on Italian medallions. Holbein's delicate touch as a painter is manifest in the gleam of the silk fabric and the porcelain quality of the flesh tones, which contribute to the harmony of the painting.   *BB*

Master of the Stalburg Portraits
(active ca. 1500)
Portraits of Claus Stalburg and his Wife Margaretha von Rhein, 1504
Inv. Nos. 845, 846
Tempera and oil on fir,
189 x 56 cm each

An ensemble of paintings, unique in its time, was commissioned for the private chapel of the Stalburg family. It included nearly life-size, full-length individual portraits of Claus Stalburg and his wife, which were painted on the inner side of the two wings flanking the altar. The centerpiece, depicting the Crucifixion, was destroyed in a fire in 1813. The patrons' portraits were intended as a showy self-representation of one

of Frankfurt's leading aristoratic families. The style of the unknown artist reflects the influence of Jörg Ratgeb and Grünewald.   *BB*

Albrecht Dürer
(1471–1528)
Job Mocked by his Wife
Inv. No. 890
Tempera and oil on lime,
96 x 51 cm

This panel, along with its counterpart depicting two musicians (Cologne, Wallraf-Richartz Museum), was the exterior of an altarpiece, visible when it was closed. The central panel has been lost. Here, Job's patience is tested by God, who sends a series of misfortunes his way. Job withstands his trials and tribulations, sitting on a dung heap, while his wife mocks him and his friends, on the other panel, try to

Albrecht Dürer
(1471–1528)
Portrait of a Young Woman
from the Fürleger Family
wearing her hair open
Gouache on canvas,
56 x 45 cm

This portrait of a young woman praying was later retouched and varnished. Originally, Dürer applied watercolor to a fine canvas, a technique he often used for portraits. A companion painting in the Berlin Gemäldegalerie shows a second young woman from the same family with braided, pinned-up hair, holding erotically symbolic plants in her hand. They were obviously meant to be displayed together to commemorate both daughters. The sitter of the portrait in the Städel collection was destined for a spiritual life, while the second daughter was destined to marry. *BB*

cheer him up with music. The split-off inner panels with portraits of standing saints are in the Alte Pinakothek in Munich. *BB*

**Mathis Gothard Neithard,
known as Grünewald**
(ca. 1475/80–1528)
Panels of the Heller Altar depicting
SS. Laurence and Cyriakus
Inv. No. HM 36, 37 (on loan from
the Historisches Museum)
Tempera and oil on fir,
99 x 43 cm

Grünewald's panels were most probably added to an altar whose centerpiece and wings Frankfurt merchant
Jakob Heller had commissioned
from Albrecht Dürer in 1510/11. They
are masterpieces of grisaille painting in which, nearly 100 years after
the Master of Flémalle (see p. 45),
Grünewald created an almost kalei-
doscopic illusion, constantly changing the impression of what the spec-
tator perceives from painting to
painted sculpture to nature.   *BB*

Lucas Cranach the Elder
(1472–1553)
The Torgau Altar, 1509
The Holy Kinship
Inv. No. 1398
Tempera and oil on lime,
central panel 121 x 100 cm

The Torgau Altar was one of the first major commissions Lucas Cranach the Elder executed after becoming court painter to the Elector of Saxony. The wings depict the Elector Fredrick the Wise and his brother, Duke John the Steadfast, as the legendary husbands of the two youngest daughters of St. Anne. In the central panel, Anne's three husbands are depicted on a portico, the one in the middle resembling Emperor Maximilian. Thus, the sacred theme of the Holy Kinship is also a political declaration of allegiance and loyalty of the two rulers to the German Emperor. *BB*

picture its charm and character. Unlike other works on the same theme, Cranach dated and marked this one with the sign of his workshop, the winged serpent. The high quality of the painting indicates that it was commissioned by a discerning patron. *BB*

Lucas Cranach the Elder
(1472–1553)
Venus, 1532
Inv. No. 1125
Tempera and oil on beech,
37 x 25 cm

The nude subject and her mythologically legitimized eroticism lend the

**Hans Baldung,
known as Grien**
(1484/85–1545)
Two Witches, 1523
Inv. No. 1123
Tempera and oil on lime,
65 x 45 cm

Hans Baldung, known as Grien
(1484/85–1545)
The Nativity
Inv. No. 1183
Tempera and oil on lime,
92 x 55 cm

Witches were often the subject of Baldung's drawings and woodcuts, but appear only once on a panel. The way the witches are portrayed indicates that this Frankfurt painting must have been quite a showpiece, commissioned by a collector. Despite the frightening celestial phenomenon in the back, the women themselves do not appear dangerous or obscene. Instead the painting retains the aesthetic charm of a nude study. Here, Baldung was making ironic reference to his contemporaries' obsession with witches and expresses the liberal views predominant in Strasbourg, where he resided at that time. *BB*

This nocturnal depiction reduces the surroundings of the Nativity to bare minimum. Baldung represents the Birth of Christ in the light of the later events of his Passion. The Christ Child, effusing ethereal light and bearing a facial expression of suffering, appears astoundingly adult. His swaddling clothes are gathered around him like a loin cloth. The angel is posed as if he were already holding the corpse of the crucified Christ (as is the case in the Angel's Pietà). The painting gives the distinct impression that Baldung was trying to find a counterpoint to the usual interpretation of the Nativity.   *BB*

ures and pictorial space blend into a festive staging of the Nativity. Just as the Three Magi are cloaked in lavish, embroidered brocade robes festooned with cords and tassels, the architectural ruins appear overgrown with rampant vines.   *BB*

Lucas Cranach the Younger
(1515–1586)
Portrait of
Philipp Melanchthon, 1559
Inv. No. SG 349
Tempera and oil on wood,
transferred to canvas,
81 x 60 cm

In his portrait of the humanist and reformer Philipp Melancthon, Cranach the Younger attempted to overcome the classic problem of portrait painting so often addressed in art criticism—that the artist was able to capture the physical but not the spiritual qualities of his subject. Here, to counteract this, Cranach contrasts Melancthon's spirituality and somewhat untidy physical appear-

Albrecht Altdorfer
(ca. 1482/85–1538)
The Adoration of the Magi
Inv. No. SG 452
Tempera and oil on lime,
110 x 78 cm

In this late work by Albrecht Altdorfer, the most important representative of the Danube School, the fig-

ance with the results of his spiritual aspirations: In his hands is a book containing the writings of Church Father Basil the Great as well as Melancthon's own epigrams—a book that is the product of the artist's imagination which his sitter holds upside down, so the observer can read it. *BB*

Conrad Faber von Creuznach

(ca. 1500–1552/53)
Double portrait of
Justinian von Holzhausen
and his Wife
Anna von Fürstenberg, 1536
Inv. No. 1729
Tempera and oil on lime,
69 x 98 cm

Conrad Faber was the portait painter of choice among Frankfurt's patrician families in the first half of the 16th century. This double portrait commissioned by the humanist Justinian von Holzhausen of himself and his wife stands out from the many, often rather formal portraits Faber painted of the members of the Holzhausen, Stralenberg, and Stalburg families. In a complete departure from the tradition of the time, Faber introduced young Amor between the two figures. Amor offers his arrow of love and a grapevine symbolizing fertility to the man and his wife, thus functioning as the allegorical link between them and conveying the artist's message that love is the force behind the marital relationship between the two spouses. *BB*

Early Netherlandish Painting

Robert Campin (ca. 1375–1444)
(Master of Flémalle)
Madonna and Child,
St. Veronica, Trinity
Inv. No. 939, 939A, 939B
Tempera and oil on oak,
160 x 68 cm; 152 x 61 cm;
149 x 61 cm

The three panels believed to have come from the Belgian town of Flémalle in Maastal show the Virgin nursing the Christ Child, St. Veronica with the cloth bearing Christ's image and the Trinity. They count among the most important and most mysterious works of Early Netherlandish painting. In the 19th century the anonymous painter of these works was named the "Master of Flémalle" after the town thought to have been the origin of his major works. It was not until the 20th century, however, that art historians were able to identify the artist as Robert Campin from Tournai, who was Rogier van der Weyden's teacher. Experts had previously believed that the panels depicting St. Veronica and the Trinity had been the front and back panels of the wings of an altarpiece. Now it is clear that both are independent and once were part of a larger ensemble. Early Netherlandish panel and altar painting was still in its infancy, however, when the

Flémalle panels were painted, so it has been difficult to determine the works to which they originally belonged; they may have come from a folding altarpiece with double wings. The monumental conception and intense psychological representation of the painted figures, as well as realistic detail of the visible world with its symbolic overshadowing rank Robert Campin's Flémalle panels with the van Eyck brothers' masterpiece, the Ghent Altarpiece. JS

15th century. It was created around 1430, at about the same time the van Eyck brothers painted the Ghent Altar. Inferior copies of Campin's great altarpiece have survived, and in these the middle panel shows the Deposition, while the two wings to the right and left depict the two thieves. This existing fragment, which constituted only the upper half of the right wing, gives some idea of the monumental effect that the lost work must once have had in its entirety. JS

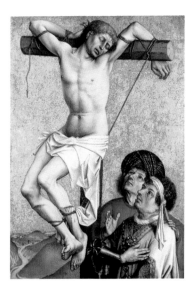

Robert Campin (ca. 1375–1444)
(Master of Flémalle)
Fragment of a wing of a triptych
depicting the Bad Thief
to the Left of Christ
Inv. No. 886
Tempera and oil on oak, 134 x 93 cm

Robert Campin's grandiose representation of the body of one of the two thieves crucified along with Christ, painted in gruesome detail, is all that remains of the most important Netherlandish altarpiece of the

Rogier van der Weyden
(1399/1400–1464)
Medici Madonna
Inv. No. 850
Tempera and oil on oak,
62 x 46 cm with the original frame

Shortly after his return from a pilgrimage to Rome in the jubilee year 1450, the Brussels artist Rogier van der Weyden was commissioned to paint a devotional picture for the Florentine banking family Medici. Sever-

al elements of the composition indicate this prestigious commission. First, the *sacra conversazione* theme dominating the picture was rare in the North; second, the lily coat of arms of the city of Florence; and third, the choice of saints depicted with the Virgin were associated with the Medici family. SS. Cosmas and Damian, the holy physicians, were the patron saints of the Medicis, and Pietro and Giovanni de'Medici, two leading members of the family, were named after SS. Peter and John.   *JS*

Jan van Eyck (ca. 1390–1441)
Lucca Madonna
Inv. No. 944
Tempera and oil on oak,
66 x 50 cm

No other painting by Jan van Eyck conveys such an immediate sense of intimacy between the observer and the figure represented as the *Lucca Madonna*, named after one of its earlier owners. In addition to the insightful observation of the emotional relationship between mother and child, the masterful use of light and shadow and, above all, the apparently incidental but in fact highly sophisticated depiction of space in the painting create this effect. The precious oriental carpet on the floor continues into the perceived space, just as the windows piercing the walls and the rib vault of the ceiling of the throne room extend beyond the frame. The observer does not experience this picture as if viewing a theatrical scene, as is the case with the Madonna panel by Petrus Christus. Instead, the viewer is drawn into the very space in which the Virgin and Child are present.   *JS*

Petrus Christus
(ca. 1415–1475/76)
Madonna and Child with
SS. Gerome and Francis, 1457
Inv. No. 920
Tempera and oil on oak,
47 x 45 cm

This Madonna by Petrus Christus ranks high among the works of Early Netherlandish painters. It marks the first time that an artist from the Netherlands succeeded in composing a picture, with mathematical perspective, according to the rules of geometry. In the tradition of Jan van Eyck he signed and dated the painting with pride, on the lower step of the throne: PETRUS CHRISTUS ME FECIT 1457 ("Petrus Christus made me in 1457"). JS

Hans Memling (ca. 1440–1494)
Portrait of a Man Wearing a High
Red Hat
Inv. No. 945
Tempera and oil on oak,
42 x 31 cm

Hans Memling came from Seligenstadt on the Main but moved to Bruges in his youth, where he soon established himself as a painter of altarpieces and religious scenes. He was also quite successful in the field of portraiture, becoming one of the most sought-after, fashionable portraitists in the Netherlands at the end of the 15th century.   JS

Hugo van der Goes
(ca. 1440–1482)
Madonna and Child
Master of Bruges (?) 1480/90
Left wing: William van Overbeke
with St. William
Right wing: Johanna de Keysere
with St. John
Inv. No. 802

Tempera and oil on oak,
the central panel in its original
frame,
30 x 23 cm

Toward the end of the 1480s, Willem van Overbeke and his wife Johanna de Keysere asked an unknown artist to convert and expand a painting of the Madonna in their possession into a small folding altar. Hugo van der Goes had painted the *Madonna and Child* some ten years earlier, which is how the unusual double frame for the center panel came into being. The phrase "en esperance," repeated on the framework several times, possibly refers to a vow made by the patron couple, who are shown on the wings of the small triptych.   JS

Master of the Tiburtine Sibyl
(active 1470–1490)
The Prophecy of the Sibyl of Tibur
Inv. No. 1068
Tempera and oil on oak,
69 x 86 cm

Hieronymus Bosch
(ca. 1450–1516)
Ecce Homo
Inv. No. 1577 (SM-V)
Tempera and oil on oak,
71 x 61 cm

Here, the Sibyl of Tibur explains to Emperor Augustus that the strange celestial phenomenon is announcing the Birth of Christ. This scene has been used throughout history as the Western counterpart of the Adoration of the Magi from the East; both honor the newborn Christ Child. The Master of the Tiburtine Sibyl named after this painting, emphasized the eternal relevance of the occurrence by setting the scene in an inner court of a castle in the Netherlands and dressing the participants in contemporary clothing. JS

Bosch painted his version of Christ before the people for a large patron family that is shown in the lower corners of the picture. These figures were damaged and painted over in either the 16th or 17th century. The remains of the figures, now visible again, were uncovered just a few years ago. The difference in the size of the figures reflects their relative importance. The children are rendered much smaller than the father and one son, whose tonsure identifies him as a monk. The Latin inscription also attributed to him is a prayer

for the patron: SALVA NOS CHRISTE REDEMPTOR ("Save us, Christ the Redeemer"). JS

event from the beginnings of Christianity but illustrates as well the correct use of devotional works of art such as itself. JS

Gerard David
(ca. 1460–1523)
St. Gerome in the
Wilderness
Inv. No. 1091
Tempera and oil on oak,
31 x 22 cm

This small panel by Gerard David from Bruges shows St. Gerome and a lion in a forest landscape. The Cardinal and Church Father is kneeling in penance before a panel painting of the Crucifixion. Using this "painting within a painting" as a reference, the small picture from around 1510 serves not only as a depiction of an

Master of Frankfurt
(active 1480–1520)
Triptych with the Crucifixion,
SS. Nicholas and Margaret along
with the patron family
Humbracht
Inv. No. 715
Tempera and oil on oak,
central panel 118 x 77 cm

This triptych of the Crucifixion came
to Frankfurt at the beginning of
the 16th century. The patron family
Humbracht had direct business
contacts with Antwerp, where the
anonymous artist lived. Still, he is
known as the Master of Frankfurt because of the number of works attributed to him in the German city. Following the practice of the time, the
male members of the family are depicted on the left, along with St.
Nicholas, the father's patron saint.
His wife and daughters are shown
on the right, under the protection of
St. Margaret.   JS

Quentin Massys
(1465/66–1530)
Portrait of a Scholar
Inv. No. 766
Tempera and oil on oak,
69 x 53 cm

With great immediacy Quentin
Massys portrays a scholar who appears to have suddenly discovered
an important truth in the book he is
reading. The rich landscape in the
background reflects the Antwerp
tradition, but the influence of Italian
portraiture on the lively composition
is equally apparent.   JS

Joos van der Beke van Cleve
(ca. 1485–1540/41)
Triptych depicting the
Lamentation of Christ
Inv. No. 803
Tempera and oil on oak,
central panel 114 x 84 cm

In 1524 the Cologne merchant and town councilor Gobel Schmitgen commissioned this altarpiece for the northern side altar of St. Maria Lyskirchen, his parish church in Cologne. The lavishly dressed patron is shown at the left edge of the central panel, and his family crest can be seen at the top of the left wing. Joos van Cleve was an obvious choice for this commission, as he was one of the earliest Antwerp artists of his time to complete such work for export.   JS

The Brunswick Monogrammist
(ca. 1525/50)
Scene from a Brothel
Inv. No. 249
Tempera and oil on oak,
33 x 46 cm

The artist, known only as the Brunswick monogrammist, worked in Antwerp from 1525 to 1550. His genre-like pictures made him the best known precursor of Pieter Brueghel and appear to capture spontaneous moments from everyday life. This painting was partially painted over in the late 16th century; the original version levied strong criticism against the church. Where now a country squire stands next to the bed of a prostitute, the artist had originally portrayed a Franciscan monk. His tonsure is still visible to the naked eye under the repainting.

JS

Netherlandish Baroque Painting

Bartolomäus Breenbergh
(1598–1657)
The Martyrdom of St. Laurence, 1647
Inv. No. 621
Oil on canvas,
87 x 103 cm

Bartolomäus Breenbergh, along with Cornelis van Poelenburch (1594/95–1667), Andries Both (1612–1641), Jan Asselijn (after 1610–1652), Nicolaes Berchem (1620–1683), and G.B. Weenix (1621–1660/61) was one of the earliest painters in the Netherlands to become an Italianist. These artists moved to Rome between 1620 and 1640. Breenbergh went to Rome in 1619 and is documented as having returned to Amsterdam in 1633. This painting is one of the most complicated compositions of his mature Amsterdam period. A seemingly unending number of figures lead the eye into the distance showing an imaginary view of Rome. The influence of Titian, Elsheimer, and Michelangelo blend freely in the figures to produce new forms, just as the various depictions of Trajan's Column, Sant'Angelo, and the church of St. Peter redefine the landscape of Rome, creating views that exist only in the artist's imagination. Despite this approach, Breenbergh succeeded in painting visions of ancient Rome that very much appealed to his contemporaries and formed the basis for many popular engravings.   *MG*

Frans Hals (1581/85–1666)
Portrait of a Man
and a Woman, 1638
Inv. Nos. 77, 78
Oil on oak, 95 x 71 cm each

These portraits, once thought to be of Rubens and his first wife, are among the most valued in Städel's collection. Hals painted the unknown couple during his most mature and most prolific artistic period. With just a few brushstrokes he succeeded in characterizing two well-to-do Dutch citizens. The man is reserved and proud; the woman has a mischievous smile and appears self-confident but at the same time approachable. *MG*

Although the child is festively clothed like an adult, this sensitive portraitist succeeds in capturing the naive curiosity in the direct glance of his subject, who cannot be more than a few years old. The panel has been cut out and extended on each side, indicating that it once was part of a larger composition. *MG*

Jacob Gerritsz. Cuyp (1594–1651)
Portrait of a Boy in a
Straw Hat with Red Lining
Inv. No. 230
Oil on oak, 37 x 32 cm

Cornelis de Vos (1585–1651)
Portrait of Susanna de Vos, 1627
Inv. No. 763
Oil on oak, 80 x 56

The sensitive portrait of the artist's chubby-cheeked daughter, born in 1626, is one of his most successful paintings. The artist, who specialized in children's portraits, captured the irreverent stubbornness of the child who, in having to sit still for the portrait, clearly pitted her strength against her father's.   *MG*

Aert van der Neer
(1603/04–1677)
Nocturnal Landscape of a Canal with Fishing Boats
Inv. No. 1092
Oil on oak, 35 x 49 cm

With shimmering lights and subtle colors, night scenes such as this prove van der Neer a master of this genre. However, the prolific landscape painter from Amsterdam was less than successful during his lifetime. This painting is one of several of his works in the Städel collection. *MG*

Ruysdael's later period, from which this is an example, that the compositions show greater resolve and more distinctive use of color. At the same time, these later works show the influence of the artist's nephew, Jacob van Ruisdael (1628/29–1682), the most important second generation landscape painter from Holland. *MG*

Salomon van Ruysdael
(ca. 1600–1670)
Ferry on a Canal, 1664
Inv. No. 100
Oil on oak, 51 x 69 cm

Along with Jan van Goyen (1596–1656) and Esaias van de Velde (ca. 1591–1630), Ruysdael was one of the founders of Dutch landscape painting. At first glance, it is difficult to distinguish the works of these artists from one another. It is not until

Aelbert Cuyp (1620–1691)
Flock of Sheep in a Meadow
Inv. No. 1107
Oil on oak, 49 x 47 cm

Cuyp painted this work around 1650/52, when he was at the height of his creative talent. Although it has never been determined that Cuyp had been to Italy, this painting approaches the style of Holland's Italianists. His atmospheric landscapes are full of light and bear a closer resemblance to the work of Claude Lorrain than do most of his Italianist contemporaries who had lived in Rome. The warm, glowing golden tone of this landscape is flooded with sunlight yet is misty at the same time. The depth is emphasized by the dark foreground with the shepherd, dog, and hut to the right. *MG*

easily recognizable on the horizon. With the barest of details and a limited palette of colors, Ruisdael succeeds in capturing the melancholy mood of a winter day, overshadowed by snow-filled clouds. The theme here is not the gay, winter ice festivities as seen in the works of Hendrick Averkamp (1585–1634), Isack van Ostade (1621–1649), or Lucas van Valckenborch (before 1535–1597); rather it addresses the inexorable, ice-cold forces of nature.   *MG*

Jacob van Ruisdael
(1628/29–1682)
Dune Landscape with Fence
Inv. No. 1240
Oil on oak, 44 x 36 cm

Ruisdael painted the dune landscape typical of Haarlem's environs many times. In this small composition of very few visual elements, the light penetrating the stormy clouds plays the crucial role. The real theme of this painting is capturing the ephemeral quality of such a fleeting moment. The ruined plank fence also serves as a symbol of transience.   *MG*

Jacob van Ruisdael
(1628/29–1682)
Winter Landscape near Haarlem
with a Lantern Post
Inv. No. 1109
Oil on canvas, 37 x 32

This small, winter landscape depicting a frozen scene near Haarlem is one of the most impressive winter views that Ruisdael painted in the 1660s. Haarlem's St. Bavo church is

Rembrandt Harmensz. van Rijn
(1606–1669)
Portrait of Margaretha
van Bilderbeecq, 1633
Inv. No. 912
Oil on oak, 68 x 55

The simple composition and contrasting light and shadow, giving the face a sculptural quality, clearly indicate this portrait is from Rembrandt's first Amsterdam period. A companion piece, the portrait of Margaretha's husband, Willem Burchgraeff, painted in 1635 by Daniel Mytens (ca. 1590–before

This is Rembrandt's most violent painting and, at the same time, one of his largest canvases. In addition to the blinding of Samson, Rembrandt shows the triumph of Delilah, who revealed the secret of her lover's superhuman strength to the Philistines. Rembrandt's original idea—to portray Samson at the moment of the attack, falling backward toward the observer from a brightly lit space to a darkened one—may be one of the reasons for the 30-year-old artist's rise to fame in Amsterdam. The powerful movement of the figures as well as the painting's format indicate an artistic debate with the work of Rubens, Rembrandt's only competitor during this period. Here he already exceeds Rubens in the extreme effects of light and shadow, the almost unbearable drama of the act, and his attention to the emotional state of his subjects—as illustrated by the expression on Delilah's face. *MG*

1648), is known to exist but has disappeared. The frame is one of the very rare original frames from the period. *MG*

Rembrandt Harmensz. van Rijn
(1606–1669)
The Blinding of Samson, 1636
Inv. No. 1383
Oil on canvas, 205 x 272 cm

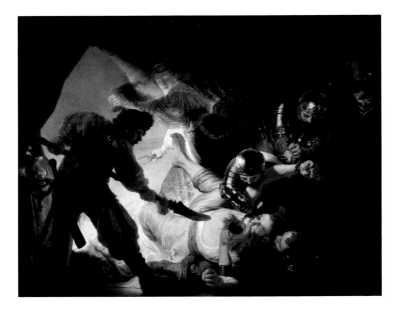

Rembrandt Harmensz. van Rijn
(1606–1669)
David Playing the Harp before Saul
Inv. No. 498
Oil on oak, 62 x 50 cm

This early painting, created around 1630, was the first Rembrandt in the Städel collection. It demonstrates that the artist was already capable of representing an ancient biblical tale

in a new and relevant fashion. Here he emphasizes the very moment in which King Saul, listening to David playing the harp, feels the first pangs of his burgeoning jealousy of the younger man. Saul will eventually kill himself, clearing the way for David's succession. *MG*

Aert de Gelder
(1645–1727)
Self-portrait as Zeuxis, Painting an Ugly Old Woman, 1685
Inv. Nr. 1015
Oil on canvas, 142 x 169 cm

Rembrandt's last student of significance chose an obscure anecdote from the life of Athenian painter Zeuxis (5th century BC) for the subject of his self-portrait. In his *Schilderboek*, published in 1604, Karel van Mander tells the story of Zeuxis choking on his uncontrolled laughter as he painted a wrinkled old woman

from a live model. The anecdote is better known as told by Cicero and Pliny. In their version, Zeuxis has the most beautiful women in the city model for a painting of Helen of Troy and selects the most perfect detail from each one in order to create an ideal portrait. In choosing van Mander's version, de Gelder may have been responding to Rembrandt's critics, as well as to his own, because they attacked the artists for their uncompromising realism that included ugliness along with beauty. *MG*

Gerard ter Borch (1617–1681)
Lady with a Wine Glass
Inv. No. 1055
Oil on canvas, 38 x 28 cm

Here, ter Borch had his younger sister Gesina model for him, as she did for many paintings on a variety of themes. The wine, letter, writing materials, and the bed with its drawn curtains in the background indicate an intimate but at the same time chaste love relationship, which the

artist leaves unexplained. The young woman's features reveal nothing of her feelings. Has she received good news, or is she drinking because her lover has forsaken her? *MG*

Gerrit Adriaensz. Berkheyde
(1638–1698)
City Hall in Amsterdam
Inv. No. 1051
Oil on canvas, 63 x 54 cm

Much like his brother Jop Adriaensz. (1630–1693), Gerrit also painted topographically precise scenes, especially of his home city, Haarlem. Further subjects of his pictures include Heidelberg, Cologne, The Hague, and of course Amsterdam, whose City Hall on the Dam was the mightiest municipal building north of the Alps. Another of his subjects was the Amsterdam Stock Exchange (compare to the painting by Jop, Städel Inv. No. 536) and other views of the city in similar works that are now equally famous. *MG*

Jan Vermeer van Delft (1632–1675)
The Geographer, 1669
Inv. Nr. 1149
Oil on canvas, 53 x 47 cm

The scholar is bending over the maps in his study. His left hand rests on a book; his right hand holds a compass. The other objects around him, especially the globe on top of the cupboard, identify him as a geographer. Although his gaze is directed toward the window, he is not distracted by something he sees outside. His facial expression and his posture indicate that he has just arrived at some important insight following a phase of concentrated contemplation. Vermeer was capable of capturing moments of psychological truth, such as this one, with great sensitivity. He is also the most outstanding colorist and painter of light of his period. This painting, as is often the case with Vermeer, is primarily based on blue, yellow, and red pigments. The room is flooded with a cool, clear light, despite the many dark shadows. They characterize the composition as well as the auxiliary lines that reinforce the perspective. *MG*

Jan van Goyen (1596–1656)
The Sea at Haarlem, 1656
Inv. No. 1071
Oil on oak, 40 x 54 cm

This masterpiece, painted in the last year of the artist's life, is evidence of the specific developments in Dutch landscape painting up until the middle of the 17th century, to which van

Goyen greatly contributed. The flat seascape, the high sky crucial to the mood and composition of the painting, and the atmospheric dampness, so typical of Holland, create a new harmonious unity.   *MG*

Adriaen Brouwer (1605/06–1638)
The Bitter Tonic
Inv. No. 1076
Oil on oak, 48 x 36 cm

In this nearly life-size picture of a man—painted in the last years of Brouwer's life—the artist altered and intensified his brushwork, reflecting a clear influence by Rubens. This, along with the subject matter, elevated the work to one of the major examples of Dutch peasant genre painting. With the most economical means, Brouwer captured the short moment of human sensory perception—the grimace that the man makes after sampling an apparently vile-tasting drink. The picture is not a mere representation of the sense of taste within a series of paintings illustrating "the five senses," which was a popular convention at the time, but proves to be the highest form of observation of a human condition. Here, Brouwer was successful in creating one of the most impressive renderings of emotion of this period.   *MG*

Jan Steen (1625/26–1679)
Moses Striking Water from the Rock
Inv. No. 1096
Oil on oak, 54 x 44 cm

In addition to Steen's familiar genre paintings (*Scene from a Tavern*, *The Alchemist*), the Städel owns this intriguing religious painting based on Exodus 17, 1–7. Today, this picture is no longer considered to be a late work but one that was executed in Haarlem around 1653 and influenced by Jacob de Wet the Elder (ca. 1610–1671/72), under whom Steen was probably studying that year. The proof is in de Wet's painting on the

same subject (Warsaw National Museum), the composition of which is almost identical: the man riding a donkey emerging at precisely the same place from the grotto; the theatrical lighting reminiscent of Rembrandt; the peasants in the foreground; and the figure of Moses, placed on a higher level in front of the dark cliff. *MG*

David Teniers the Younger
(1610–1690)
Smoker in a Rural Tavern,
1636 (?)
Inv. No. 1040
Oil on oak, 32 x 47 cm

David Teniers the Younger was the successful and prolific artistic heir of Adriaen Brouwer (1605/06–1638). In 1651 Teniers was appointed court painter to Archduke Leopold Wilhelm in Brussels. This is typical of Tenier's style and demonstrates his ability to reproduce with extraordinary accuracy the texture and surface qualities of various objects: glasses, glazed stoneware mugs, and polished copper pans. Most of these objects appear in the fore-

ground in order to feature his painting skill. At the same time he masters the easy, flowing brushstrokes of Rubens, visible in the diffused light of the background.   *MG*

Peter Paul Rubens (1577–1640)
The Betrothal of St. Catherine
Reverse side: Battle of Horsemen
(Double-sided painted oil sketches)
Inv. No. 464
Oil on oak, 63 x 50 cm

This small oil sketch from Städel's collection was part of Rubens' design for the 5.64-meter-high altar of the St. Augustine hermitage church in Antwerp (1525/26–1528). In this early, possibly first color sketch, Rubens brings together SS. Nicholas, Laurence, Augustine, Sebastian, and George, along with a series of female saints leading up to St. Catherine, shown receiving the Christ Child from the Virgin, in a magnificent High Baroque *sacra conversazione*. With few, fleeting brushstrokes, Rubens lays the groundwork for coloration and shading, as well as all the other decisive qualities of the composition, which are also evident in the giant altar (today in the Museum of Fine Arts in Antwerp). *MG*

Peter Paul Rubens (1577–1640)
(and workshop)
Dido and Aeneas
Inv. No. 2097
Oil on canvas, 214 x 294 cm

Rubens depicts the meeting of the Trojan hero who was to become the founder of Rome and the Queen of Carthage. The subject is taken from Virgil. The painting captures the moment in which the Queen, who has sworn eternal fidelity to her murdered husband Sychaeus, is over-

come by love for another man. During a hunt in honor of her guest, everyone is forced to flee a sudden storm. Dido and Aeneas take refuge in a cave. Here, Rubens illustrates the scene in which Aeneas lifts Dido from the saddle and initiates the tragic love story. While Aeneas answers the call of the gods, Dido commits suicide. The monumental historical painting may have come from the royal collection at the Alcazar in Madrid. It is the last large work that was acquired for the Städel Baroque collection. *MG*

Roelant Savery (1576/78–1639)
Orpheus among the Animals, 1610
Inv. No. 977
Oil on oak, 51 x 66 cm

The myth of Orpheus, a popular theme in the history of painting, provides this work with an excuse to depict a variety of different animals. Savery was one of the leading painters of animals in this period, and because of his interest in zoology was appointed to the Hapsburg court, at the service of Rudolf II in Prague from 1604 to 1614. New dis-

coveries in botany and zoology were initially recorded and spread through the graphic arts (for example, by Georg Hoefnagel, 1542–1600). Savery modeled his work on Hoefnagel's precise drawings and painted most of the animals in profile, as Hoefnagel did. This blending of scientific naturalism with the forest landscape of the Netherlands is evident in the work of Gillis van Coninxloos (1544–1607), which foreshadowed the later development in Netherlandish painting, whereby the reality of the visible world was captured and reproduced with great precision. _MG_

The Städel collection has four signed and dated works by this Flemish landscape painter, who spent ten years at the court of Matthias of Austria in Linz. In 1593 he came to Frankfurt, where he died four years later. The painting from 1573, _Animal Pasture Under the Trees_, is a noticeably modern and original composition in which Valckenborch almost eliminates the usual Flemish three-colored combination of brown, green, and blue for the fore-, middle-, and background respectively, in favor of more natural color tones and shading. The delicate colors glimpsed between the trees add a unique effect to the scene. The second painting illustrated here, the winter landscape in Antwerp, is more dependent on color and tone contrast in capturing the atmosphere of a clear, cold winter day. _MG_

Lucas van Valckenborch
(before 1535–1597)

Animal Pasture
Under the Trees, 1573
Inventory No. 1221
Oil on oak,
35 x 47 cm

A View of
Antwerp with the
Frozen Schelde, 1590
Inventory No. 668
Oil on oak,
43 x 64 cm

Italian, French, and Spanish Baroque Painting

Giovanni Battista Crespi, known as Il Cerano (1575–1633)
The Baptism of Christ, 1601
Inv. No. 1527
Oil on canvas, 203 x 255

Crespi was the most important artist in Milan around 1600. He was painter, architect, and sculptor to Cardinal Francesco Borromeo, who was the cousin and successor of the influential Archbishop Carlo Borromeo, a staunch opponent of the Reformation. The cardinal carried on the missionary and charitable work started by the archbishop. Crespi spent the 1590s in Rome and also perhaps went to Venice before finally returning to Milan in 1600/01, possibly

with Francesco Borromeo. *The Baptism of Christ*, painted in 1601, contains elements of Mannerist art but the forms of Early Baroque art are also clearly evident. The Mannerist elements include the almost violent torsion of the Christ figure with the head in an unconventional, tilted position; the delicate, shimmering colors of the angels' robes, among the most elegant to be found in Italian painting around 1600; and the course of the river, which takes an abrupt plunge on the left along the lower edge of the painting. The landscape that fills the background betrays a knowledge of the works of Jan Breughel the Elder, who was also employed by Francesco Borromeo,

and Paul Bril, also active in Rome. The figure of St. John would evoke the solidity of Rubens's figures, were it not for the conspicuous and extreme modeling of the body, proof that Crespi was also a talented sculptor.   *MG*

Pompeo Girolamo Batoni
(1708–1787)
Allegory of Art, 1740
Inv. No. 731
Oil on canvas, 175 x 138 cm

Batoni is the last significant Italian artist from Rome, famous for his portraits of English aristocrats on the "Grand Tour." His cool, polished style is classical but also appropriate for his rarer allegorical paintings. In this work he depicts the five liberal arts. "Painting" occupies the center; to her right is "Poetry," playing a lyre. "Music" is next to her, with a double flute. In the lower left is the half-nude figure of "Sculpture" next to a bust of Emperor Hadrian and the tools of her craft.

She holds a hammer in her right hand and is linked to "Painting" with her left. "Architecture" is in the background with a protractor and a compass. The painting's charm lies in its elegance and the unforced interaction among the figures of the group. *MG*

Giovanni Battista Tiepolo
(1696–1770)
The Saints of the Crotta Family
Inv. No. 1441
Oil on canvas, 195 x 320 cm

This large canvas was painted during Tiepolo's most important and productive period. It was probably executed either directly before or shortly after the completion of his major work, the painting of the interior of the Episcopal Palace in Würzburg (1750–1753). Despite the religious subject, this is not an altar painting. All of the principle figures are ancestors of the Crotta family from Bergamo, who had gained prominence and wealth in Venice but were not among the ranks of Venetian nobility. The foremost purpose of this painting, which originally was displayed in the Crotta Palace, was to document the venerable heritage of the family, presenting the most important events of the family's history as if on a stage. The religious conversion of Bergamo is brought about through the martyrdom of St. Alexander, the city's patron saint. St. Grata, an ancestor still revered there, presents Alexander's severed head to Lupus, her father, who was the city's ruler at the time and who had ordered Alexander's execution. Instead of blood, beautiful flowers spring from the martyr's wound, a miracle which ultimately results in the conversion of Lupus and his wife Adelaide. SS. Fermus and Rusticus, two elegant young men shown holding palm branches, are also ancestors of the Crottas who suffered martyrdom on another occasion. Tiepolo executed this complicated commission with an elegant and balanced composition of a colorful, magnificent scene. *MG*

Attributed to
Pietro Longhi (1702–1785)
Traveling Actors in front of the
Doge's Palace in Venice
Inv. No. 1529
Oil on canvas 59 x 72 cm

This painting is a typical example of the special way Longhi and the artists of his studio depicted scenes from everyday life in Venice towards the end of the 18th century. Itinerant entertainers present their earthy humor from an improvised stage under the arcade of the Doge's Palace. The performance appears to be some sort of romantic comedy, and some of the spectators are masked. During the carnival the boundaries between various social strata seem to disappear, and Longhi makes no difference in the way he portrays the masked revelers who are on their way to a ball, somewhat indignant at the interruption, and the simple people enjoying the performance. Not only was Longhi a sharp observer and chronicler of his time, but he was also the most talented painter of the Venetian Rococo. His highly discriminating use of color and incomparably delicate brushwork bring to life the materials and textures depicted and reinforce the carefully observed gestures and facial expressions of his subjects. *MG*

**Bernardo Bellotto,
known as Canaletto**
(1721–1780)
View of the Bacino di San Marco
Inv. No. 851
Oil on canvas, 77 x 97 cm

This painting shows the famous view of Venice seen from the distance of the Riva degli Schiavoni. The observer sees the scene as if it were framed by an oval window—a format Cana-

letto rarely used. The ships in the Bacino di San Marco take up the foreground, while the buildings in the distance are shown foreshortened. The eye follows the deliberate perspective deep into the Canal Grande, which opens up in the background revealing countless ship masts in the misty distance and an extraordinary wealth of detail. This is not, however, an exact topographical rendition but the product of many detailed sketches that were first compiled in the studio to form the basis for a variety of paintings.   *MG*

the tall black hat help date the painting. The subject's contemplative, concentrated look is fixed on an object to the left, outside the frame. The artist's skill can be seen in the way he deals with the man's prominent nose. This is an intimate and quiet portrait, typical of the circle of artists around court painter François Clouet (1522–1572). This painting was in Johann Friedrich Städel's original collection.   *MG*

French Master
(active 1560–1590)
Portrait of a Young Man
Inv. No. 279
Oil on wood, 37 x 27 cm

This sensitive portrait of a man, dressed in the Spanish fashion popular in the late 16th century, shows the subject in three-quarter view against a gray background. The irregularly pleated white collar and

Nicolas Poussin (1593–1665)
Landscape During a
Thunderstorm with Pyramus
and Thisbe
Inv. No. 1849
Oil on canvas, 193 x 274 cm

This is Poussin's largest landscape, painted for the Roman palace of Cassiano del Pozzo, the artist's most important patron in Rome. Recent research has revealed that the stormy landscape and the strictly symmetrical composition were the result of many changes and an almost total repainting of the picture. The changes include the oval lake in the center that divides the surface of the canvas, the dark gray sky overshadowed by the storm, the dramatic lighting, as well as the subject of the painting itself. It is the tragic story (taken from Ovid's *Metamorphosis*) of two lovers from Babylon who were not meant to be together. In an attempt to meet secretly outside the gates of the city, they lose their lives through a tragic misunderstanding. Few paintings reveal Poussin's efforts to solve the problems of form and content as clearly as this landscape does.   *MG*

Claude Gellée, known as Lorrain
(1600–1682)
Christ Appears before
Mary Magdalene
(Noli me tangere), 1681
Inv. No. 1479
Oil on canvas, 85 x 41 cm

Claude Lorrain, who worked exclusively in Rome, painted this biblical landscape in the last year of his life. According to Christian tradition, Mary Magdalene met Christ early on the morning of the Resurrection at the open grave before the gates of Jerusalem. The recent restoration of the painting has now revealed the extraordinary atmosphere of this time of day. The colors are again cool and silvery, and the various elements and

figures in the composition are illuminated by the light of the rising sun, giving them a sculptural clarity. The early morning mist rises over the strips of land, and over the houses in the city, leading the eye all the way to the coast. The restoration also revealed the elongated body proportions of Christ and Mary Magdalene, typical of Lorrain's later work. In an earlier restoration these proportions had been painted over and altered. The companion piece, *Landscape with St. Philip Baptizing the Eunuch*, was painted in 1678 and is now in the National Gallery of Wales in Cardiff.

MG

Jean-Baptiste-Siméon Chardin
(1699–1779)
Still Life with Partridge
and Pear
1748
Inv. No. 2129
Oil on canvas, 39 x 46

This painting was created following a phase in which Chardin exclusively produced genre pictures. It is difficult to categorize because it contains only a few subject elements: the bird, the looped string for transporting it, and the pear. Is it a kitchen painting or a hunting still life? Chardin's individual style is clearly visible here. The tabletop, the pear, and the fluffy breast feathers of the bird create almost abstract planes of color in the flat light. The eye is challenged to sort these into a harmonious composition, and this—the active participation of the observer—is crucial to understanding Chardin's painting. Denis Diderot (1713–1784) aptly described this process of perception: "Come closer and everything blurs, flattens, and disappears; step away and everything is recreated and regenerated." (Salon of 1763). *MG*

Jean-Antoine Watteau (1684–1721)
The Pilgrimage to the
Island of Cythera
Inv. No. 2150
Oil on canvas, 44 x 54 cm

Watteau painted three versions of this scene. The version he painted for admission to the Academy became a milestone of 18th century art and is now in the Louvre. In 1717 it earned him the title of "Peintre de fêtes galantes," which the academy newly created just for him. The second variation, painted just a short time later, is in the Charlottenburg Palace in Berlin. The third version, now in the Städel, was painted around 1710 but rediscovered much later. It was in this version that Watteau had given the theme of the pilgrimage to Cythera his first serious consideration. Watteau's Flemish origin is still recognizable in the

painting, along with the influence of Claude Gillot, his teacher in Paris between 1703 and 1707. It is also clear that theater influenced the artist. *Les trois cousines*, a popular musical comedy that appeared at the Comédie Française, was probably the inspiration for the delicate, costumed figures in the foreground, on their way to the island of love.   *MG*

Jean-Baptiste Pater (1695–1736)
Country Festival
Inv. No. 1772
Oil on canvas, 49 x 59 cm

Jean-Baptiste Pater, Jean-Antoine Watteau's (1684–1721) only student, continued the tradition of the *fêtes galantes* in countless paintings without ever achieving the level of realism that characterizes Watteau's

work. Pater's smooth painting style lacks the lively brushwork of his teacher. This painting does, however, exhibit the typical erotic charm that Rococo art so valued.   *MG*

Diego Rodriguez de Silva y Velázquez
(1599–1660)
Portrait of Cardinal Borja
Inv. No. 1045
Oil on canvas, 64 x 48 cm

Gaspar de Borja y Velasco (1582–1645) was the Archbishop of Seville and Toledo, Primate of Spain, as well as Philipp IV's temporary ambassador to the Vatican. Velázquez painted his portrait during his stay in Toledo from 1643 to 1645, shortly before the cardinal's death. There are several versions of the portrait,

Francisco de Goya y Lucientes
(1746–1828)
Two Scenes from the Spanish War
Inv. No. 1980, 1981
Oil on wood, 31 x 40 cm each

Painted with quick, fluid brush-strokes, the horrific scenes belong to a series of six similar wooden panels. They were part of the settlement in the separation of property in Goya's family following the death of the artists's wife in 1812. On the notary's list of items that ultimately went to Goya's son, Xavier, they were designated "X9" ("X" for Xavier and "9" for the number assigned to this group of paintings), and their designation was added in white oil paint to the lower left edge of each panel. Goya made these oil sketches around the same time that he was producing the paintings and prints belonging to the series he called *The Horrors of War.*   *MG*

all of which exhibit the same folds in the vestments. But a copy in London shows Borja, full-length, sitting in a chair. A drawing by Velázquez in the Academia de San Fernando in Madrid most closely resembles the version of the portrait which is now in the Städel collection.   *MG*

German Baroque Painting

Paul Juvenel the Elder (1579–1643)
The Baptism of Christ, 1609
Inv. No. 1667
Oil on wood, 99 x 88 cm

The artist probably submitted this signed and dated painting as his masterpiece to the city council in Nuremberg in 1609, because he had painted an unsigned and undated version of it, called *Baptism in the Jordan*, earlier the same year. Juvenel's son was also born in 1609, which means that he must have traveled to Italy sometime before this date. This would explain the influence of Adam Elsheimer (1578–1610) and his Roman contemporaries on Juvenel's early works. The group of figures in the lower right, for example is used to exhibit the striking contrasts of light and shadow which typify Elsheimer and his group. Later Juvenel achieved fame with his many paintings on the facades of buildings.   *MG*

Adam Elsheimer (1578–1610)
The Frankfurt Altarpiece of the
Exaltation of the True Cross

Central panel:
Exaltation of the True Cross
Inv. No. 2024

Surrounded by six scenes from
the search for and discovery of
the cross:
The Embarkation of Empress Helena
Inv. No. 2131 (SM-V)
The Interrogation of the Jew
Inv. No. 2142
The Excavation of the Cross
Inv. No. 2118 (SM-V)

The Testing of the Cross
Inv. No. 2140 (SM-V)
Emperor Heraclius's Entry into
Jerusalem on Horseback is
Forbidden
Inv. No. 2119 (SM-V)
Heraclius Carries the Cross into
Jerusalem Barefoot
Inv. No. 2054

Oil on copper,
Central panel 49 x 35 cm;
Side panels approx. 23 x 15 cm
Predella panels approx. 15 x 16 cm

The Deluge, Inv. No 1607, oil on copper, 27 x 35 cm

Adam Elsheimer (1578–1610)

The Städel owns ten paintings by Adam Elsheimer, forming the most comprehensive collection of original works by the best known of Frankfurt's painters. Among these works is Elsheimer's masterpiece, the Frankfurt *Altarpiece of the Exaltation of the True Cross*, as well as *The Deluge*, the *Conversion of St. Paul*, and *Jacob's Dream*. Three further attributed paintings on copper include one from Städel's collection, entitled *The Road to Emmaus* and the pair of paintings depicting Mercury and Argus and Nymph and Satyr. These round off the main focus of this collection.

Within just 30 years (1950 to 1981) the museum succeeded in recovering the altar that had been documented in old sources but was believed to have been lost. The shape of the altar is a modern reconstruction based on authentic sketches from 1612 to 1619 that have survived. The central panel was the first part of the altar that the Städel collection acquired in 1950. It shows the feast of the Exaltation of the Cross (September 14). The raised Cross is in the center, surrounded by a multitude of saints, figures from the Old and New Testaments, and a gathering of angels. In the upper left, the brightest part of the painting, Elsheimer depicts the Coronation of the Virgin. The remaining six copper panels tell the story of Empress Helena's search and recovery of the true Cross and its return to Jerusalem. It is the best example of Elsheimer's mature miniature painting style. The colors are dazzling, the composition extraordinarily confident. Even the features of the least important figures are fully characterized. The altar was created in Rome, probably between 1605 and 1608/09 and belongs to Elsheimer's later work.

The Deluge is an earlier painting, depicting a dark scene with great contrast. It shows the drama of the destruction of humanity in the biblical flood. This work also features an important characteristic of Elsheimer's painting—he loved nocturnal scenes. In this painting the Venetian influences of Tintoretto (1518–1594) and Jacopo Bassano (active 1535–1592) are obvious, which is why it has been dated around 1600, shortly after Elsheimer's arrival in Rome.

Jacob's Dream, another early work, shows that Elsheimer was one of the Flemish artists who brought landscape painting to Italy. The minutely detailed forest on the left resembles the style of Gillis van Coninxloo (ca. 1544–1605). The valley on the right, with its rich detail including the barely discernible mill, is evidence of Elsheimer's talent for this form of painting for which Flemish artists were famous. Coninxloo spent a short time in Frankenthal near Worms, where Elsheimer may have met him and other Flemish landscape painters. Later, in Rome, Elsheimer and Paul Bril (1554–1626) had a great influence on their contemporaries, including Claude Lorrain.   *MG*

Jakob's Dream, Inv. No. 2136, oil on copper, 20 x 26 cm

Georg Flegel (1566–1638)
Still Life with Bread and Sweets
Inv. No. 2055
Oil on wood, 22 x 17 cm

Confectionery items first appeared as the subject of still lifes around 1600, when the import of sugar cane gradually replaced honey as a sweetener. Candied sugar, also known as "ice sugar," originated in Madeira or in the Canary Islands. In this tiny painting from his late period, Flegel exhibits technical skill and his talent as a keen observer. He expertly renders the characteristics of various materials and depicts different ways of preparing candied fruit. To the right are two figs with a sparkling, crystalline sugar crust. The bowl contains candied fruit topped with powdered sugar. Paintings depicting such luxury goods were popular among Frankfurt's well-to-do burghers, but the symbolism in Flegel's pictures was intended to qualify this attraction with a religious and moral message. MG

Abraham Mignon (1640–1679)
Still Life with Autumn Fruit
Inv. No. 121
Oil on oak, 35 x 45 cm

Here, Frankfurt-born artist Abraham Mignon has created a rich still life of autumn fruit with pewter dishes and glasses filled with wine. The painting is the product of Mignon's studies in Utrecht, where he moved in 1669. Although he originally studied under Jacob Marell (1614–1681) in Frankfurt, Mignon was predominantly influenced by his teacher in Utrecht, Jan Davidsz. de Heem (1606–1683/84). In 1876 Mignon returned to Frankfurt, where Maria Sybilla Merian (1647–1717) became his pupil, but he remained true to the Dutch tradition of still life painting. MG

Johann Heinrich Roos (1631–1685)
Family of Roman Shepherds with their Flocks, 1674
Inv. No. 555
Oil on canvas, 45 x 61 cm

Germany's most important animal and landscape painter of the late 17th century spent the last years of his life (after 1667) in Frankfurt, where he met with great acclaim painting the idyllic, bucolic scenes

Anton Kern (1710–1747)
Rinaldo and Armida in the
Magic Forest
Inv. No. 2094
Oil on wood, 58 x 82 cm

that were his specialty. This picture comes from that period and reflects the new type of representation that Roos had adopted in Amsterdam, where he was influenced by Karel Dujardin (1622–1678), Cornelis de Bie (1621/22–1664), and the paintings of the Italianists. Here the wide flat landscape of Holland is replaced by the hills of the *campagna* outside of Rome, where antique ruins bask in the Mediterranean sunlight. Roos had never been to Italy, but he knew how to present Dutch tradition with a new romanticism. *MG*

The popular scene from Torquato Tasso's epic poem "Jerusalem Delivered" shows Rinaldo in the grove of the sorceress Armida. He listens to the sounds of the viola da gamba and the flute, played by Armida's companions, but refuses to succumb to the music or to Armida, who emerges from the bark of the myrtle tree. To combat temptation, Rinaldo defends himself steadfastly with sword and shield. The relaxed brushwork and the choice of colors show the influence of Giambattista Pittoni (1687–1767), with whom Kern studied in Venice from 1724 to 1731. Given the similarities to a painting done at the same time by Pittoni, Kern probably executed this in Venice before moving to Rome in 1738. The cool colors of Pittoni and the graceful postures of the figures support this theory. *MG*

German Master (active ca. 1700)
Portrait of a Girl Dressed as a
Shepherdess and Portrait of a
Boy in Hunting Attire, 1665
Inv. No. 26, 37
Oil on canvas,
86 x 68 cm; 87 x 68 cm

These two attractive, colorful
children's portraits were painted by
an unknown artist who signed his
paintings AvD. The paintings were
probably destined to be part of a
room decoration. Judging from the
coat of arms they bear, the portraits
could be of members of the influential Schönborn family. If one accepts
the date, which along with the signature was added later, the portraits
could be of the future Bishop of Bam-
berg and Archbishop of Mainz, Elector and Chancellor, Lothar Franz von
Schönborn and his sister. In 1665 he
would have been ten years old. *MG*

Franz Anton Maulbertsch
(1724–1796)
The Four Elements, design for
a ceiling decoration
Inv. No. 1622
Oil on canvas, 47 x 69 cm

Along with a second smaller version now in the Austrian Gallery of
the Lower Belvedere in Vienna, this
sketch was part of Maulbertsch's
first large commission (1750–52) to
paint the ceiling of the ceremonial
hall of Kirchstetten Palace in Lower
Austria. After considerable experimentation, he finally developed his
own individual style in early works
such as this. Although this picture
is purely allegorical, the three principle figures display an unusually
high level of motion and emotion,
as well as "unmistakably human
qualities, earthy and solidly rooted
in genre painting." (K. Garras,
1974)   *MG*

**Johann Martin Schmidt, known as
Kremserschmidt** (1718–1801)
Pietà
Inv. No. SG 599
Oil on canvas, 55 x 43 cm

Johann Martin Schmidt belongs to
a group of German historical painters, active at the end of the 18th
century. The most important of
these artists were Franz Anton
Maulbertsch (1724–1796), Bernhard
Rode (1725–1797), Januarius Zick
(1730–1797), and Johann Christian
Thomas Wink (1738–1797). All were
enormously prolific, imaginative
and demonstrated a change of di-
rection in German painting in favor
of the style of Rembrandt's late
works. They borrowed from Rembrandt's strong contrasts of light
and shadow and his free brushwork.   *MG*

Januarius Zick (1730–1797)
The Adoration of the Shepherds
and the Presentation of Jesus
in the Temple
Inv. No. 1198, 1199
Oil on canvas, 89 x 126 cm

The eclectic but original style of Januarius Zick is far more evident in his panel paintings than in the numerous profane and religious fresco commissions which made him especially popular during his lifetime. He was most strongly influenced by 17th-century Dutch painting, but also by Italian and French Baroque painting, to which he had been exposed during his stay in Paris in 1757 and his visit to Rome in 1758/59. His stylistic development

ranges from Rococo to sensitive Classicism. He is valued more for his painterly skill than for his interpretation of subjects common to this period.   *MG*

ideal landscapes, which follow the Romantic tradition of Claude Lorrain, made him one of the most popular landscape painters in Rome.   *MG*

Jakob Philipp Hackert (1737–1807)
View of St. Peter's in Rome, 1777
Inv. No. 1551
Oil on canvas, 72 x 90 cm

In 1769, one year after his arrival in Rome, Jakob Philipp Hackert made a drawing of the Tiber River and St. Peter's Basilica as seen from the Ponte Molle. In 1770 and 1771 he completed two paintings of the same setting. In the latter version in the Städel, the view is considerably reduced and the Dome of St. Peter's has been emphasized to become the central motif. Hackert's

Johann Heinrich Wilhelm Tischbein
(1751–1829)
Goethe in the Roman Campagna
Inv. No. 1157
Oil on canvas, 164 x 206 cm

This portrait was painted in 1787 in Rome during Goethe's Italian travels. The famous German poet had stayed in the painter's house on the Corso, and although he mentioned this painting several times in his writings, Goethe never actually saw it completed. Tischbein shows Goethe as a man of the world, surrounded by antique ruins including a relief of the tale of Iphigenia, a reference to Goethe's work of the same name, which he had just completed. German painter Ludwig Strack aptly characterized Tischbein's portrait: "The eye of the philosophical poet registers amazement at this change in nature and in human things, and the horrible realization of the transience of all things is discernible in his features," Interestingly, the painting better served the fame of the poet than the painter. Artistic flaws such as the highly irritating two left feet (!) of the subject may be explained by the fact that the picture was left incomplete for a very long time. It is still unknown exactly when or even by whom the painting was actually finished. *MG*

19th-century Painting and Sculpture

Joseph Anton Koch (1768–1839)
Landscape with Noah,
Offering a Sacrifice of
Gratitude
Inv. No. 767
Oil on canvas, 86 x 116 cm

Josef Anton Koch transformed the conventional landscape painting of his time by combining the Italian landscape style with the idyllic, heroic vision of Poussin. His work greatly influenced the younger German artists working in Rome. This early piece, painted at the beginning of the 19th century, is Koch's first independent oil painting. The figures were executed by his friend Gottlieb Schick (1776–1812). *HJZ*

Franz Pforr (1788–1812)
The Count von Hapsburg and the Priest, 1810
Inv. No. 959
Oil on canvas, 46 x 55 cm

The subject of this painting was common and had even supplied the material for one of Friedrich Schiller's

(1759–1805) ballads. Pforr's painting is one of the first historical pictures of this genre, which was very popular in the 19th century. The opposites of count and priest, altar boy and squire, and horses and hounds are joined before a landscape that is clear and perfectly executed to the minutest detail. Rudolf von Hapsburg dismounts and turns his horse over to the priest, who carries the Blessed Sacrament.   *HJZ*

Carl Philipp Fohr (1795–1818)
The Waterfalls of Tivoli
Inv. No. 805
Oil on canvas, 74 x 105

Carl Philipp Fohr was commissioned to paint this picture by Frankfurt Merchant Philipp Passavant. He painted it in 1817 in the studio of Anton Koch, his teacher, who was working on a painting of Tivoli at the time. The tri-level construc-

tion and clear composition of this work, the diversity of its motifs, and the lively auxiliary figures clearly indicate Koch's influence. Fohr painstakingly worked out each single motif—the Spanish chestnut in the foreground, the picture of Mary, the sleeping figure, the spinner with the little boy—through countless sketches he prepared on walking tours with Philipp and Johann David Passavant.   *IE*

Johann (Jean) David Passavant
(1787–1861)
Self-portrait in a Beret in front of a Roman Landscape
Inv. No. 1585
Oil on canvas, 45 x 32 cm

Johann David Passavant painted this impressive self-portrait in 1818 in Rome. From 1815 to 1817 he studied with Jacques-Louis David and Antoine-Jean Gros. From 1817 to 1824 he remained primarily in Italy,

ders befit her station in life and indicate a degree of prosperity without detracting from the natural charm of the painting. The portrait was commissioned by Marie's husband, Alfred, Baron von Bernus, who was the most important patron of the Nazarenes in Frankfurt. The painting, however, is in no way an example of the movement. Veit avoids all reference to symbolism and underlying meaning, focusing the viewer's interest on the face of the subject, who was optimistic and known for her zest for life.   *SS*

where he had contact with the Germans living in Rome. After 1824 he returned to Frankfurt, devoting himself increasingly to aesthetics and art history, and became Inspector of the Städel Art Institute from 1840 to 1861. The portrait marks a transitional period in Passavant's work. The head with its clear gaze is still painted in the tradition of French Classicism, while the background shows the strong influence of Anton Koch's German-Roman school of landscape painting.   *IE*

Philipp Veit (1793–1877)
Portrait of Baroness von Bernus,
1838
Inv. No. 1798 (SM-V)
Oil on canvas, 129 x 97 cm

"Like the Queen of Beauty on her throne" (Karl Koetshau), sits the newly married Marie, lost in thought, her face turned toward the light. Her festive gown and the splendid fur stole around her shoul-

Friedrich Overbeck (1789–1869)
The Triumph of Religion in the Arts
(The Magnificat of the Arts)
Inv. No. 892
Oil on canvas, 392 x 392 cm

This painting, which served as summary of the Nazarene philosophy, borrows its composition from Raphael's frescos in the Stanza della Segnatura in the Vatican. Friedrich Overbeck's complex composition serves to illustrate the Nazarene

premise that art is only justified when it serves religion. The Mother of God, surrounded by figures from the Old and New Testaments, appears in heaven. Artists from the Middle Ages through the Renaissance are assembled on earth. They range from Raphael, Leonardo da Vinci, and Michaelangelo to Dürer, Holbein, Schongauer, and the van Eyck brothers. Further, the Emperor and Pope are depicted as ideal patrons of the arts. The Städel commissioned this painting, which Overbeck took 11 years to complete. When it arrived in Frankfurt in 1840, it met with great acclaim, as the profane and realistic depiction of historical subjects in painting had become popular and fashionable in Germany.   *HJZ*

Caspar David Friedrich
(1774–1840)
Landscape with the "Rosenberg"
in Switzerland
Inv. No. 1821
Oil on canvas, 35 x 49

As confirmed by landscape studies from 1898, the panorama that appears here in the wan light of early morning is the view from the great Winterberg mountain to the Bohemian mountain ranges of the Kaltenberg and Rosenberg. Caspar David Friedrich encountered these three summits during a hike he took in May, 1808, and recorded his impressions in a four-part pencil drawing which has survived to the present. Friedrich was fascinated by the three

Carl Blechen (1798–1840)
Women Bathing in the Park
of Terni
Inv. No. 1888
Oil on canvas, 104 x 78 cm

mountain's symbolism of the Holy Trinity and succeeded in transforming this inconspicuous landscape, veiled by early morning mist, from a picture of a nature scene to a symbolic painting. The subtle nuance of the coloration bears testimony to his masterful technical ability to capture the moods of nature, despite the fact that Friedrich never actually finished this painting because of a stroke he suffered in 1835. *IE*

Carl Blechen's tumultuous life, characterized by contrasting influences and numerous artistic experiments, culminated in a trip to Italy in 1828/29. He was fascinated by both the Mediterranean countryside and the natural way of life. On his return journey he discovered the motif for this picture, which he captured in four small studies and four large paintings. Here, the preparatory drawing was not filled in with color. Instead, color, light, and shadow were directly applied to the canvas. *HJZ*

Carl Spitzweg (1808–1885)
The Widower, 1844
Inv. No. SG 328
Oil on canvas, 58 x 67 cm

Arnold Böcklin (1827–1901)
The Honeymoon
On loan from the German state
Tempera on wood, 72 x 53

This painting is an example of the narrative genre painting of Carl Spitzweg's early period. A plump, well-to-do burgher is shown in his Sunday-best suit, sitting on a bench in front of a park setting that resembles a stage backdrop. With curiosity he observes two ladies as they stroll by. Far too obviously he exhibits the props of his state of mourning. In his hands he holds a large handkerchief and a cut-out silhouette profile of his deceased wife. The subject of this painting is not the lonely grieving widower, but the humorous insight of the artist into the very human foibles of his protagonist. The piece evokes associations with burlesque Biedermeier folk theater, which is reinforced by the theatrical composition and the exaggerated lighting falling on the widower like a spotlight. *IE*

The title of this work and its subject are closely associated with the marriage of Arnold Böcklin's daughter Clara to Peter Bruckmann on July 6, 1876, in Florence. In contrast to an earlier version from 1875 and a later version from 1878, Böcklin concentrates in this painting on the two lovers rather than on their integration into the Italian landscape, which serves more as a backdrop for a piece of human drama: The two sit dangerously close to the edge of a boulder. The bridegroom tenderly addresses his young bride, his right hand resting on her shoulder. With his left arm he points to the distant landscape that holds their happy future, while Clara directs her gaze at the deep, peaceful valley. The romantic scene is rounded off by a sunbeam, falling onto Clara's optimistically stretched out tiptoe. *IE*

Hans von Marées (1837–1887)
Two Seated Children
Inv. No. 1987
Oil on wood
91 x 83 cm

Hans von Marées turned to monumental panel painting while he was in Italy in 1878. This picture was actually part of a triptych painted in Florence, depicting the legend of SS. Martin, Hubertus, and George

(Bavarian State Painting Collection, Neue Pinakothek, Munich). The painting of the two children, with its moody ambience, was originally part of a painted frieze of six putti which ran along the base of the larger work. The names of the saints were to appear on separate panels along the upper edge. The execution of the enormous piece was long delayed. In 1887, the year he died, Marées was still working on the ensemble, which is now divided among several locations. All that now remains is a crayon drawing showing the original placement of the saints, the children, and the framing. Konrad Fiedler acquired the painting from the artist's estate and framed it in this original Renaissance frame. *IE*

Charles-François Daubigny

(1817–1878)
French Orchard at
Harvest Time
(Le verger), 1876
Inv. No. 1444 (SM-V)
Oil on canvas, 168 x 300 cm

This large canvas is one of Charles-François Daubigny's major works and was the last painting he exhibited in the Salon of 1876. It shows a peaceful corner of an orchard, drenched in the sunlight of a late autumn afternoon, full of fruit-laden apple trees in the Île-de-France. The large format invites the observer to plunge into the thick, unkempt undergrowth and become a part of this convincing and superbly rendered depiction of nature. *HJZ*

Eugène Delacroix

(1798–1863)
Arabian Fantasy
(Fantasia arabe), 1833
Inv. No. 1466 (SM-V)
Oil on canvas, 60 x 75 cm

In 1832 Eugène Delacroix visited Morocco in the entourage of the Comte de Mornay, a journey that so profoundly influenced him that he continued painting oriental subjects up until his death. This picture comes alive through the suspenseful contrast between the wild group

of riders charging in from the right and the immobile figure of the Bedouin in the left foreground. *HJZ*

Jean-Baptiste-Camille Corot
(1796–1875)
View of Marino, near Albano (A Marino, près Albano, aspect général)
Inv. No. 1498
Oil on canvas, 23 x 35 cm

Corot visited Marino in the Albano mountains toward the end of 1826 and again in May, 1827. He painted the city and its surroundings early in the morning, creating the fleeting impression of the landscape with rapidly applied, broad brushstrokes and little attention to detail. Despite this, the city is recognizable by the mass of its buildings capped by the bell tower. The sun is still low on the horizon, so that the shadows dominate the valley in the foreground, while the eye takes in the expanse of the plateau in the background. With great economy the painting thus gives an accurate reproduction of the scene. *HJZ*

Gustave Courbet (1819–1877)
View of Frankfurt with the Old
Bridge from Sachsenhausen
Inv. No. SG 1140
Oil on canvas, 54 x 78 cm

For the young Gustave Courbet, Frankfurt was an important stop on the way to fame. As early as 1852 he showed his paintings in the Lederfabrik (Leather Factory), before submitting them to the Salon in Paris. In Frankfurt, *The Burial at Ornans* (Musée d'Orsay, Paris) caused a furor, and Courbet became the talk of the town. At the invitation of the Frankfurt Art Association Courbet moved to the city on the Main river, where he would remain for almost one year. At first he worked in the Städel art school, then moved into a shared studio in Kettenweg. He greatly influenced the local artists Victor Müller (1839–1871), Otto Scholderer (1834–1902), and Carl Goebel (1824–1899). Courbet made an early mark for himself as a portrait painter of the city's wealthy society. He also left behind this unusual view from the Deutschordenshaus, across the Old Bridge to the Frankfurt cathedral. Unlike the views

from the west, painted by Christian Morgenstern (1805–1867) or Domenico Quaglio (1787–1837), which focus on the distinctive silhouette of the narrow, winding lanes of the old town, Courbet alters the cityscape here by presenting it from an everyday perspective. *SS*

Otto Scholderer (1834–1902)
The Violinist at the Window, 1861
Inv. No. SG 320
Oil on canvas, 150 x 103 cm

This is one of Otto Scholderer's major works, painted in Frankfurt shortly after the artist's first trip to Paris and his association with Gustave Courbet (1819–1877). Although the window motif usually appears in the smaller, intimate format used by Romantic painters such as Moritz von Schwind (1804–1871) and Caspar David Friedrich (1774–1840), Scholderer consciously chooses this monumental format for a profane subject. A young man holding a violin sits on a window sill, lost in thought and looking dreamily into the distance. He has lowered the instrument; the bow points towards sheets of musical notation lying on a chair in the room. The music has faded away. No sound disturbs the private atmosphere of the interior. The subject of this painting is neither music nor the outer world as seen through the open window. It is the state of contemplation of the young man, whose introspection is mirrored in his reflection in the window. *IE*

Louis Eysen (1843–1899)
Still Life with Shell, Water Glass, and Spoon, 1869
Inv. No. SG 637
Oil on cardboard 23 x 48 cm

Only in Paris could his friends convince the recalcitrant artist to try his hand at painting. Louis Eysen began with still life scenes such as this one depicting a shell and a glass. Unlike Otto Scholderer (1834–1902) in his paintings, Eysen was primarily concerned here with the composition on the surface of the table and in the depth of field. The mastery of this piece lies in the way the objects are arranged and in their relationship to one another. *HJZ*

Victor Müller (1839–1871)
Flower Girl, 1871
Inv. No. SG 640
Oil on canvas, 56 x 91 cm

A dark-haired beauty with a splendid bouquet of peonies, carnations, clematis, fire lillies, and geraniums in her arms rushes through a green meadow as if fleeing the ominous, stormy sky in the background. The flower girl is Cella Berteneder (1858–1901), painter of floral motifs and later wife of artist Hans Thoma (1839–1924). Painted shortly before Victor Müller's death, this unusual picture is a cross between a sensitive portrait and decorative floral still life that symbolizes the transient beauty of youth and summer. *IE.*

Wilhelm Leibl (1844–1900)
Elderly Farmer and Young Girl
(The Unequal Couple)
Inv. No. 1340 (SM-V)
Oil on canvas, 76 x 62

In the spring of 1875 Wilhelm Leibl moved to Unterschondorf on the western shore of the Ammersee in Bavaria. There he painted portraits and genre scenes with two figures, including the one of this unequal couple. The painting depicts the old fisherman Lenz and Theresia Bauer, the step-daughter of Unterschondorf's tavern-keeper Steininger. Leibl had had a brief and unhappy love affair with her. The two figures sit close together in the corner of a rustic room, facing the observer. The old, almost toothless man puts his arm loosely around the pretty young woman. At first sight, she seems to take his importunate manner in her stride. But the impression is false. Theresia holds the glass in her right hand at such an oblique angle that she could at any moment dump its contents—thereby ending the supposed idyll abruptly. In this work, Leibl consciously refers to the long tradition of pictures showing unsuitable couples by Renaissance and Baroque painters and printmakers from Germany and the Netherlands, but he adds an anecdotal character to this work.   *IE*

Hans Thoma (1839–1924)
Holzhausen Park and Small Palace
in Frankfurt am Main, 1880
Inv. No. SG 264
Oil on canvas, 51 x 72 cm

In the winter of 1877 Hans Thoma
moved to Frankfurt with his wife Cella, his mother, and his sister Agathe.
They lived in Lersnerstrasse 20, near
the Holzhausen Park, which Thoma
printed at least four times. This version, showing the view through an
open window with the Holzhausen
Palace, is the fourth of the series,
dated 1883. Looking back years later
in 1919, Thoma described it in his
memoires as "the valid proof of the
flourishing joy of our sense of being.
(...) The painting is now in the
Städel Art Institute and says more
about the beautiful, fortunate peaceful state in which we lived than
words ever could do." This mood of
spring outside is expressed in the interior through the open Bible and
the small bouquet of forget-me-nots
on the window sill. The composition

reminds the observer of a personal
altar. Although the motif of the open
window symbolizes wanderlust and
longing in Romantic painting,
Thoma uses it here to represent
contemplation and concentration in
the foreground. The landscape in
the background symbolizes the in-
carnation of the divine in nature in
the tradition of Caspar David Friedrich (1774–1840) and Philip Otto
Runge (1777–1810), although in
Thoma's painting the subject is han-
dled with realism.   *IE*

Hans Thoma (1839–1924)
Self-portrait in front of a Birch
Forest, 1899
Inv. No. 1370 (SM-V)
Oil on canvas, 94 x 76 cm

Hans Thoma painted two self-por-
traits when he turned 60. In the one
in the Frankfurt collection, the photographic likeness of the subject
contrasts sharply with the branching
birch trees, seen in the reddish eve-

ning light in the background. Calm and questioning, Thoma faces the observer with clear eyes, as though he were summing up things at the height of his career. The same year he was called to Karlruhe by the Grand Duke of Baden and appointed director of the Kunsthalle and professor of the art school there. Thoma painted his self-portrait before a landscape that he had previously painted with his wife Cella—a rare example of a joint work by an artist couple. He pays hommage to Städel Director Henry Thode with the ring that he wears on his right hand, shown supported by a walking staff. The ring bears the inscription "with a will to be yourself" and was a gift, in admiration and friendship, from Thode to Thoma.   *IE*

Friedrich (Fritz) von Uhde
(1848–1911)
Christ with the Disciples in Emmaus
Inv. No. 1200
Oil on canvas, 76 x 62 cm

This is the second of Friedrich von Uhde's religious paintings. It was completed in 1884 shortly after a painting called *Let the Children Come unto Me*, which is in the Musem of Fine Arts in Leipzig. It captures the moment when two of Christ's disciples recognize the resurrected Son of God in a man they had mistaken for a stranger. Uhde sets the biblical tale in a rustic room in the late 19th century. While Christ appears in his long, traditional robe, his disciples wear simple, contemporary cloth-

ing. The presentation of this sacred event in a profane and impoverished environment, along with the depiction of Christ meeting with figures of the lower levels of society, was considered a breach of the religious convention that demands timeless and heroic depiction of religious subjects. It earned Uhde sharp criticism from his contemporaries. A circle of light resembling a halo directly behind Christ's head on the wooden walls of the room reinforce the validity of Christ's message. At the same time this painting heralds the coming of German Impressionism modeled on the work of Max Liebermann (1847–1935). One critic praised Uhde for his "pleasant, coloristic advances."   *IE*

Edvard Munch (1863–1944)
In the Tavern, 1890
Inv. No. SG 365
Oil on canvas, 65 x 71 cm

According to information obtained from the artist, this painting was made during Edvard Munch's stay in France in the winter of 1889/90. It shows a tavern in the Parisian suburb of St. Cloud, near the Seine. The main figure, a crude looking man, stands isolated and indecisive in the center of the composition. Uncertainly, he hides his right hand in his trouser pocket. His shoes are exaggerated, so large that they make him appear to be a caricature. The bearded barkeeper, leaning with his elbows on the bar, eyes the man mistrustfully. A tense atmosphere pervades, which is intensified by Munch's characteristic coloration in broken tones. The conscious carelessness of the representation along with the individual facial expressions of the protagonists clearly show the influence of French painter Jean-François Raffaëlli (1850–1924), whose socially critical paintings and writings inspired Munch to portray not only contemporary society but also the psychology of his subjects. In this and other works similar to the literary trend at the time, Munch created a panorama of socially disadvantaged outsiders.   *IE*

Max Liebermann (1847–1935)
The Orphanage Courtyard in Amsterdam (Free Period in the Amsterdam Orphange)
Inv. No. 1351 (SM-V)
Oil on canvas, 79 x 108 cm

Starting at 8:30 the girls had to sew and knit. Between noon and 1:30 p.m. they could rest, then it was back to work until 6:30 p.m. Strict rules were enforced in the Burgerweesenhuis. Max Liebermann needed special permission to observe and sketch his subjects during their midday recess. Despite the many studies he did on site, this is not a snapshot of everyday life in the Amsterdam orphange; the painting originated in Liebermann's Munich studio. There the chestnut tree was "planted" in the middle of the courtyard to cast its dance of sun spots. Local girls modeled as orphans, posing with one of the picturesque costumes that Liebermann had purchased during his first stay in Holland in 1876 for later use in his pictures. Its colors were symbolic: Black stood for the orphans' grief at having lost their parents, red for the love of Amsterdam's citizens who protected them. The newly founded Städel Museum Association made this early example of German plein air painting its debut purchase in 1899, thus casting a vote for civil social involvement as well as for pure art.   *SS*

Lovis Corinth (1858–1925)
Carmencita (Portrait of Charlotte Berend-Corinth in Spanish Dress), 1924
Inv. No. 2064 (SM-V)
Oil on canvas, 130 x 90 cm

Carmencita is the last of the series of portraits that Lovis Corinth painted of his wife Charlotte Berend-Corinth, who was 23 years his junior. One

Gustave Courbet (1819–1877)
The Wave
Inv. No. 1433 (SM-V)
Oil on canvas, 63 x 92 cm

The list of Gustave Courbet's works shows some 60 paintings of whirlpools, flood and ebb tides that he painted between 1865 and 1869 on the Normandy coast and which he later completed in his studio. They are the expression of man's struggle to survive and at the same time symbolize political renewal and hope; they are nature studies and also milestones on the way toward abstraction in the history of art. The reduction in subject matter is quite extreme: There is no sign of man; no land is in sight. The observer stands before the unrestrained force of nature and has no fixed place of retreat, drawn into the surf against the breakers. At the same time the eye takes in the entire expanse of the water, leaving the viewer to feel deserted and abandoned. *SS*

year before his death he painted his wife dressed as Carmen as she returned from a costume party of the Berlin Secession. He applied the paint quickly and confidently, with a sure hand and a feeling for the strong contrast between black, white and red. Shapes and boundaries blur. In this mature late work, the subject serves only to generate art for art's sake. *HJZ*

Claude Monet (1840–1926)
The Luncheon
(Le Déjeuner),
1868
Inv. No. SG 170
Oil on canvas,
232 x 151 cm

Contemporary critics were fascinated by the "modern light streaming through the curtains," as they saw Claude Monet's *Déjeuner* at the first Impressionist exhibition at Nadar in Paris. But how was the painting to be categorized? Its subject was too

banal to be considered historical, too monumental in size to be an illustration of an interior, too lively for a still life, and too fleeting for a portrait. Monet quite clearly did not follow the rules of genre and would have to pay for this break of tradition. The jury turned down his painting when he submitted it for the annual Salon in 1870. This was a great disappointment to the artist, who had hoped that precisely this kind of bourgeois subject matter would secure his future. During the months that he had worked on this painting, in the winter of 1868, he had settled in Etretat and for the first time had enough portrait commissions to earn a steady living and keep a roof over his head. There he dreamed of security and happiness with Camille and little Jean. It was this familiar environment that the modern artist hoped would provide him with subjects. He stepped down from the pantheon of artists and found his place among middle-class society, which welcomed its new arrival.   *SS*

Edgar Degas (1834–1917)
Orchestra Musicians
(Musiciens à l'orchestre)
Inv. No. SG 237
Oil on canvas,
69 x 49 cm

Although Edgar Degas exclusively devoted himself to historical subjects and portraits until the 1860s, from that period on he concentrated on small to middle-sized genre scenes from everyday life. He painted *Orchestra Musicians* in 1870/71, shortly after completing *L'orchestre de L'Opéra*, which is now in the Musée d'Orsay. From its inception the painting now in the Städel was plagued by the artist's self doubt. In 1874 he asked its owner at the time, baritone Jean-Baptiste Faure, to return it to him so that he could rework it. As X-rays confirm, Degas cropped the painting on three sides and added about one-third to the upper edge of the canvas. These changes document the way Degas worked and attest to the modernity of the artist, who was able to conceive such a daring view. He reveals the contrast between the colorful, glittering world of the ballet stage and the dark zone occupied by the musicians in their orchestra pit. This sharp contrast is intensified by the variation in the lighting, in the scale of the composition, and in the painting technique. The orchestra musicians are painted in the style of the Old Master with smooth brushwork and intricate detail, and the dancers with fleeting, vibrating brushstrokes. The heads of the musicians, which dominate the foreground, and the

The position of the *Dancer* contrasts sharply with the typical works of contemporary schooled sculptors who saw in this figure a breach of the classical rules of balance. She stands on her left leg, stretching her left hand out to the side. Simultaneously, she reaches behind her back with her right hand to hold the foot of her right leg, which is sharply bent backward. Between 1900 and 1910 Edgar Degas produced a series of figures showing variations of this position, in an attempt to find a sculpted translation for this condition of imbalance. The bronze casting conveys the impression of the lively modeling in soft wax that was layered in thumb-size portions onto the figure until its shape was firmly established. All the characteristics of motion are replicated. At the same time the individuality of the dancer represented disappears behind the standardization of the surface. *GM*

stems of the string instruments, which were added later, join the two planes of the painting. *IE*

Edgar Degas (1834–1917)
Dancer Holding her Right
Foot in her Right Hand
(Danseuse tenant son pied
droit de sa main droite)
1900–1910
Inv. No. SGP 63
Bronze, height 53 cm

Edouard Manet (1832–1883)
The Croquet Party
(La partie de croquet)
Inv. No. 1476 (SM-V)
Oil on canvas, 73 x 106 cm

A game of croquet is in progress in the garden of Belgian artist Alfred Stevens. The ladies are about to start their turn while the gentlemen casually observe. Edouard Manet has traded his mallet for a paintbrush. His colleague Paul Roudier has taken his place as the fourth player but has yet to participate actively and remains uninvolved in the background. The lady about to drive the ball is Victorine Meurent, whom Manet had already painted nude as *Olympia* and in *Déjeuner sur l'herbe* (Musée d'Orsay, Paris). In *The Croquet Party* she appears middle class and sporty. In 1873, when the picture was painted, croquet was a popular leisure activity in which both sexes could participate informally. Manet no longer found inspiration in painting nude figures and historical compositions. Along with Claude Monet he had already begun to experiment with plein air painting. The protagonists of the contemporary art scene, the artists and their models, left the cities and moved to the countryside. The garden became their studio. *SS*

Pierre-Auguste Renoir (1841–1919)
After the Luncheon
(La fin du déjeuner), 1879
Inv. No. SG 176
Oil on canvas, 101 x 81 cm

This intimate luncheon scene takes place in the leafy arbor of the Cabaret d'Olivier, the Montmartre restaurant frequented by Pierre-Auguste Renoir and his friends. The view is closely cropped and, in its spontaneity, resembles a contemporary photograph. Parisian actress Ellen André and Renoir's brother sit close together in the shade of a blooming

chestnut tree and enjoy the relaxed period after luncheon over liqueurs and cigarettes. The discrete tête-à-tête is joined by an elegant lady, dressed in black. She is one of Renoir's models whom we recognize from his earlier studies. The figures around the table are silent, caught up in their own thoughts and avoiding eye contact with each other and with the observer. The delicate colors of the glasses and carafes, the shading of the tablecloth, and the stylish clothing of the women announce Renoir's command of color that culminates in his *Luncheon of the Boating Party* (1881, Phillips Collection, Washington), the epitome of French plein air painting.   *IE*

Vincent van Gogh (1853–1890)
Farm house in Nuenen
(La Chaumière)
Inv. No. 1436 (SM-V)
Oil on canvas, 60 x 85 cm

Vincent van Gogh spent the summer of 1885 with his parents in Nue-nen in Brabant. There he painted a series of pictures showing the landscape with its straw covered roofs and its local people, mainly simple farmers and artisans. This dark composition belongs to van Gogh's early period, in which he still modeled his work on the paintings of Jean-François Millet (1814–1875) and artists of the Barbizon School and their Dutch successors.   *HJZ*

Gustave Moreau (1826–1898)
Pietà, 1867
Inv. No. 1373 (SM-V)
Oil on wood, 27 x 33 cm

The religious theme of the Pietà runs throughout the entire body of work of the French symbolists. Gustave Moreau's first representation of the Madonna with her lifeless son dates back to 1851 and is profoundly influenced by Eugène Delacroix (1798–1863). His influence is also to be found in this later work in the Städel collection. Moreau's *Pietà* emphasizes the love of the Virgin,

Pierre Puvis de Chavannes
(1824–1898)
St. Mary Magdalene in the Desert
Inv. No. 1457 (SM-V)
Oil on canvas, 157 x 106 cm

Pierre Puvis de Chavannes exhibited this painting in the 1870 Salon in Paris. St. Mary Magdalene, the patron of Provence, is shown standing barefoot in the chalk hills of the Chaîne de la Sainte-Baume, east of Marseille. According to legend, she sailed from Palestine with St. Maximin and landed in Provence, where she remained until her death. Analogous to the painting of St. Mary of

who cradles her dead son at the foot of the cross, tenderly embracing him in her arms. Her head is bent over him so that the two gold halos virtually blend into one another.   *IE*

Egypt on which Puvis de Chavannes based his work, it shows the saint as a typical penitent, with loosened hair. The skull she holds in her left hand indicates that she is engaged in a meditation on vanity. A somewhat different earlier version of the same subject is now in the Rijksmuseum Kröller-Müller in Otterlo.   *IE*

Fernand Khnopff (1858–1921)
The Game Warden, 1883
Inv. No. 1805
Oil on canvas, 151 x 177 cm

This early Symbolist work was completed in 1883, the founding year of a group of artists who called themselves "Les XX." The group's members, in addition to Fernand Khnopff, included James Ensor (1860–1949) and Théophile van Rysselberghe (1862–1926). Two years earlier, in 1881, Khnopff completed a similar painting with the programmatic title *A Crisis*, showing a lonely man against a landscape. Walther Rathenau is believed to have bought *The Game Warden* at an exhibition of the Munich Secession in 1896. Its catalogue entry (Number 207) calls it *The Watchman in Expectation*. Rathenau's mother presented it to the Städel in 1926 in memory of her son. The painting shows the game warden in profile, rooted in place, standing in a dry meadow that takes up two-thirds of the canvas. The village of Fosset is in the background. The isolated game warden is fighting a losing battle. He no longer has any connection to his surroundings and has lost his

ability to live in harmony and accord with nature. Khnopff's painting symbolizes the abandonment of mankind in a hostile world. It shows the game warden almost in silhouette, in his gray and black uniform, hat and gun, standing like a cut-out in the landscape. The dense sensuality of Gustave Moreau's paintings develops into an impenetrable, incontrovertibly human and temporal representation in Khnopff's works and ends in a timeless, imperturbable silence full of mystery and mysticism. *IE*

James Ensor (1860–1949)
Communion, 1899
Inv. No. SG 465
Oil on canvas, 57 x 53 cm

Religious subjects, skeletons, and masks pervade the works of Belgian Symbolists after 1885. The title of this painting refers to the holy sacrament of First Communion, the rite of passage that allows Catholic boys and girls to take part in the ritual Last Supper in the company of their religious community. But the stark frontal view of the girl, who is wearing a bright yellow dress, does not evoke a festive mood. Her mouth gapes in terror as if she were about to scream, and her pale face is paralyzed in fear. James Ensor depicts the defenseless child at the moment of her deliverance to the church. The grinning faces, decorated masks, and skulls emphasize the threat to her existence. With this bitter satire, Ensor exposes the pretenses of church and society as well as the restrictions and conventions they impose. *IE*

Odilon Redon (1840–1916)
Christ and the Samaritan
(Le bouquet blanc)
Inv. No. SG 1198
Oil on canvas, 65 x 50 cm

This painting was made in the late 1890s, in the heyday of the newly discovered, esoteric religious and mystical lyricism in Paris. From 1885 onwards Odilon Redon maintained close contact with the French symbolist poets, especially Stéphane Mallarmé (1842–1898). Redon's artist friends even dubbed him the "Mallarmé of Painting." Using visual reality as a point of departure, Redon created works full of fantasy and mystery. The woman with long brown hair, shown in profile, and the head of the man with closed eyes are familiar subjects that run throughout the artist's entire body of work. Enhanced by the floral forms, they blend into an unrealistic composition, remote and isolated, unified only by the opaque red-brown coloring. Redon's imagination and creativity fuse with figura-

Giovanni Segantini (1858–1899)
On the Sheep Hill of Pontresina
(Alpine Landscape at Sunset)
Inv. No. 1559
Oil on canvas, 86 x 138 cm

Toward the end of his life Giovanni Segantini worked on a large triptych that he called *La vita*, *La natura*, and *La morte*. In these Symbolist Alpine landscapes the artist created a pantheistic, excessive, mystical view of the mountains that mirror human perceptions. The painting in the Städel collection is a smaller variation of *La vita*, cropped closer and painted from another perspective. A herd of sheep is seen as it disappears over the ridge. The Bondasca mountains in the Engadine glow in the evening light, painted in Segantini's characteristic technique of placing small, strokes of paint next to each other.   *HJZ*

tive elements, resulting in a mysterious work of art. Just as undefined in space and in time, mythology of the Ancient World places the *Birth of Venus*, the Städel's second painting by Odilon Redon, in the no man's land of phantasy.   *IE*

Ferdinand Hodler (1853–1918)
Lake Geneva with the Savoy Alps
(Autumn on Lake Geneva), 1907
Inv. No. SG 1229
Oil on canvas, 50 x 40 cm

This almost abstract autumn land-scape by Ferdinand Hodler is his second version of the view of Lake Geneva with the Savoy Alps, which was painted in 1907 and exhibited in the "XI Serie" exhibition of the Zurich Art Association from December, 1907, to January 1908. The over-whelmingly horizontal composition consisting of a shore, reflections in the water, a mountain range and the sky follow the principle of Parallel-ism professed by Hodler. The har-monious interaction of line and col-or prevent the painting from appear-ing formal or static. Although Hodler's landscapes never contain human figures, they bear witness to man's yearning to be one with na-ture within a cosmic order in the universe. Shortly before his death in 1918, Hodler confessed his pan-theistic creed while gazing over Lake Geneva: "Do you see how everything back there merges into lines and space? Don't you feel as if you were standing at the edge of earth, freely associating with the cosmos? That is what I will paint in the future!" *IE*

Henri Rousseau (1844–1910)
The Avenue in Saint-Cloud Park
Inv. No. SG 404
Oil on canvas, 46 x 38 cm

The avenue bordered by lime trees draws the observer's eye deep into the picture and leads to a towering monument on the horizon. The rows of trees progress with mathe-matical precision in perfectly cen-tered perspective towards the tower, until the branches merge in the sky at the end of the avenue. In contrast to the spirited painting of the leaves

on the lime trees, the strolling figures on the avenue seem like static, estranged accessories to the composition. The shadows from the right that break up the sunlight on the path do nothing to liven these figures. The park at Saint-Cloud, on the southwestern shore of the Seine, across from the Bois de Boulogne, was the subject of many paintings by Henri Rousseau's contemporaries. In 1670 the brother of Louis XIV built a palace and the park of Le Nôtre outside the gates of the city. The Allee de la Lanterne, which ended at a monument dedicated to Napoleon I, could have been Rousseau's model for this view, as visual reality clearly inspired the self-taught artist's naïve fantasy composition. Rousseau painted what could be considered a companion piece to this painting in the same year of 1908, entitled *The Ball Players* (Solomon R. Guggenheim Museum, New York). *IE*

20th-century Painting and Sculpture

nancy, the sculpture remained unfinished, which can be seen in the face and in the agitated surface of the bronze sculpture. Rodin described this as an innovation that lead to his Impressionist sculpture. After he had abandoned his plans for the *Gate to Hell*, he exhibited *Eve* in the Salon of 1899, where it was the first large sculpture to be shown without a base.   *GM*

Charles Despiau (1874–1946)
Eve, ca. 1927
Inv. No. St.P 37 (SM-V)
Bronze, height 192 cm

Auguste Rodin (1840–1917)
Eve, 1881
Inv. No. St.P 374 (SM-V)
Bronze, height 175 cm

Auguste Rodin originally planned *Eve* as a companion piece to his sculpture, *Adam*. Each stands on a step and was meant to flank the path to the *Gate of Hell*, the name of the double bronze portal that Rodin had been working on since 1880 for the Musée des Arts Décoratifs in Paris. For the figure of Adam, Rodin borrowed from Michelangelo's design. Eve's posture reminds the viewer of the Expulsion from the Garden of Paradise on the ceiling of the Sistine Chapel in the Vatican. Due, in large part, to the model's preg-

Charles Despiau's architecturally constructed female nude figure presents a striking contrast to Auguste Rodin's *Eve* of 1881. Rodin's figure expresses the anxiety and fear following the Expulsion from Paradise. His Eve tries to cover her body with her arms. Despiau answers with the calm, smoothed plasticity of an introverted figure free of narrative gestures. Similar to Aristide Maillol (1861–1944), Despiau only shows what is pertinent. The large figure, originally planned for a monument, followed a 79-centimeter-high figure from 1925. Both Rodin's and Despiau's bronze sculptures belonged to the collection of George Harmann, who gave them to the Städel, making it possible to compare the work of the two masters, Rodin and his one-time assistant Despiau. *GM*

Pierre Bonnard (1867–1947)
Reclining Nude against a
White and Blue Plaid
(Nu Couché fond carreaux blanc
et bleus), ca. 1909
Inv. No. 2158 (SM-V)
Oil on canvas, 60 x 65 cm

Studies for this composition have not been found among Pierre Bonnard's drawings, nor among the drafts for his prints. The combination of a female body that is close to nature and the abstract plaid pattern of the surface is unusual. The torso is clearly presented in a three-dimensional space but the flat representation of the legs draws the eye of the observer outside the frame, abruptly ending the picture. In the background, however, there again is an illusion of space. In painting this nude Bonnard could

have been influenced by the work of Paul Gaugin (1848–1903), especially by his reclining nude, *Aha oe feii* from 1892 (Pushkin Museum, Moscow). The formal arrangement of the picture, however, argues against this theory and indicates that Bonnard was familiar with the paintings of Henri Matisse (1869–1954) as well as the Cubist pictorial language of Pablo Picasso (1881–1973) and Georges Braques (1882–1963). *GM*

small relief at the suggestion of Aristide Maillol (1861–1944) who had been in Essoyes in 1907 to model a bust of Renoir. In the relief Renoir borrows from the tradition of Ferdinand Levillain (1837–1905) or Henri Chapu (1833–1891) in modeling the hair, while the plastic modeling of the head shows that he was inspired by the Impressionistic sculpture of Auguste Rodin (1840–1917) and Edgar Degas (1834–1917). The individual parts subordinate themselves to the whole, and the hair reflects light on the face beneath it. *GM*

Aristide Maillol (1861–1944)
Woman with Crab, Squatting (La femme au crabe, Femme accroupie)
Ca. 1900/09
Inv. No. St.P 389 (SM-V)
Bronze, height 17 cm

Aristide Maillol consciously positioned his model to show her body in its fully developed femininity and balanced proportions without presenting her coquettishly. In a natural scene that could have been taken from a genre painting, the woman

Pierre-Auguste Renoir (1841–1919)
Coco, 1908
Inv. No. SGP 79 b
Bronze, height 27 cm

This bronze casting from the Galerie Flechtheim in Berlin was purchased by the Städel in 1929. It is the second sculpture that Renoir himself modeled and shows the head of Claude (Coco), his youngest son, born in 1901 in the family summer house in Essoyes. Several months before he made this bust, Renoir completed a

squats with her legs spread wide apart and entices a crab with her open hands that rest on the ground. The date originally given for this work was based on a preparatory sketch from 1930, but now it is clear that a casting of this bronze had already been made in 1910 for the collection of I. A. Morosov (today in the Pushkin Museum, Moscow). Later castings have added to the uncertainty, and the exact date for the completion of this work has yet to be determined. *GM*

Henri Matisse (1869–1954)
Still Life (Fleurs et céramique:
Les Capucines)
Inv. No. SG 1213
Oil on canvas 94 x 83 cm

Henri Matisse painted this still life under the powerful impression of the new compositions which Paul Cézanne (1839–1906) and, after him, Pablo Picasso (1881–1973) raised to a formal principle. The painted three-dimensional room was to be eliminated in favor of the two-dimensional pictorial surface. In Matisse's work the intimated depth of field, which is also generated through the choice of color, alternates with the objects that have become flat surfaces of color. Based on comparisons of style, this work could be dated from the period between 1911 and 1913, about the time of Matisse's second trip to Morocco. He added the signature and gave the painting its second title in 1913 when he sold it to his Parisian Galerie Bernheim-Jeune. Robert von Hirsch bought the painting from the gallery in 1917. The painting came to the Städel's Städtische Galerie under the former inventory number

SG 277. In 1937 the painting was confiscated and later sold on June 30, 1939, at an auction in Lucerne, along with Franz Marc's *Dog Lying in the Snow* (see p. 132) to Le Ray W. Berdeau of Florida. In 1962 the painting was purchased from G. David Thompson of Pittsburgh via the Galerie Beyeler in Basle and with the help of the Frankfurt Savings Bank and the Cultural Board of Frankfurt.   *GM*

Pablo Picasso (1881–1973)
Portrait of Fernande Olivier, 1909
Inv. No. (SM-V)
Oil on canvas, 65 x 55 cm

This painting, which comes from the collection of Paul Guillaume, is among the definitive works of Cubism, which Pablo Picasso (1881–1973) developed in his pictures of landscapes, people, and in a series of portraits of his companion Fernande Olivier. He painted Fernande's Cubist portrait during his sum-

mer holidays in his Spanish homeland, in the village of Horta de Ebro. He painted his subject against the village's mountainous backdrop and carried over the impression of the fissured, stony landscape to Fernande's physiognomy. The individual characteristics of her face gave way to a new pictorial surface made up of tectonic planes. Upon his return to Paris in 1909 Picasso modeled a sculpture entitled *Head of a Woman*, consisting of angular particles of the same size, which give the work a crystalline appearance of three-dimensionality. The artists demonstrated this quality in numerous preparatory sketches as well as in the painting in the Frankfurt collection.   *GM*

Naum Gabo (1890–1977)
Constructivist Head No. 1, 1915
(reconstructed in 1985)
Inv. No. St.P 439
Three layered plywood,
height 54 cm

Alexander Archipenko
(1880–1964)
The Bather, 1915
Inv. No. St.P 416 (SM-V)
Plaster and paper maché on an
inner wire frame,
height 50 cm

The Bather was Alexander Archipenko's first painted sculpture and is unique among free-standing works. Archipenko developed the technique used in its production as a result of a lack of materials suitable for sculpture available to him while he was in Cimiez near Nice during World War I. He continued to use the technique, which united painting and sculpture in synthetic Cubism, in his reliefs until his late period. Here, he built the body out of paper maché and plaster applied to a wire frame. The surface serves as the background for a standing figure of a female nude. The sculpture provides the structure for the painterly shaping of the body, which creates the il-

This female bust is constructed of interlocking planes interposed with empty spaces. The individual pieces intersect and reinforce each other. The outer contour is determined by the form of the surface, whose open structure reveals the inner space. This technique, which Naum Gabo learned when he studied in Munich, is commonly used in architectural models and industrial design. This, along with the stylistic demands of the Futurists, lead him to create *Constructivist Head No. 1*, his first stereometric sculpture, which he prepared in preliminary sketches. Commissioned to organize the first Russian art exhibition in Berlin in 1922, Gabo probably exhibited this head among other works. When he decided to immigrate to the West and traveled via England to America, he took the disassembled *Constructivist Head No. 1* with him. The sculpture remained in his possession until his death, and it remained in his family until it was sold to the Städel by the Galerie Annely Juda in London. *GM*

lusion of mass even where there is none. In the 1920s *The Bather* was already exhibited in Paris, Venice, Berlin, and Prague and originally belonged to the legendary collection of Sally Falk in Geneva.　　　*GM*

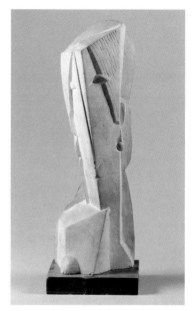

Henri Laurens (1885–1954)
Woman with Earrings
(Tête de femme aux boucles d'oreilles), 1921
Inv. No. SGP 195
Terracotta, height 37 cm

In his early work the self-taught sculptor Henri Laurens was influenced by Auguste Rodin (1840–1917) until his friendship to Georges Braque (1882–1963) directed him to Cubism. He first expressed the artistic tenets of this movement in paper collages and colored bas reliefs. This female nude is among Laurens' first Cubist sculptures, influenced by Braque and Pablo Picasso (1881–1973). The body is made up of a reduced volume of individual crystalline-shaped pieces that are broken up by round shapes such as the earrings. The sculpture is directly relat-ed to the relief *Woman with Fan* (Femme à l'éventail) from 1921 and its preparatory sketches.　　　*GM*

Fernand Léger (1881–1955)
The Fishermen (Les pêcheurs), 1921
Inv. No. 2132
Oil on canvas, 60 x 91 cm

Fernand Léger exhibited *The Fishermen* in 1928 and noted on the reverse side that it was the reworked version of a theme that appeared in three additional pictures on the same subject in the Galerie Flechtheim in Berlin. After that the painting changed hands, going through several private collections in Paris, New York and Baltimore until 1975, when the Städel acquired it through one of the museum's administrators, Werner Wirthle. It is part of a series of *"paysages animés,"* with its reduced shapes and clear structure showing the influence of Le Corbusier (1887–1965) and Piet Mondrian (1872–1944), whose works Léger adapted after the World War I. *The Fishermen* suggests a positive view of the world, an affirmation of the technical age and its constructions, to which the individual and his environment have outwardly adapted.   *GM*

Ernst Ludwig Kirchner
(1880–1938)
Nude with Hat, ca. 1911
Inv. No. SG 1168
Oil on canvas, 196 x 65 cm

According to the artist, the inspiration for this work was Lucas Cranach the Elder's *Venus* (see p. 41). Ernst Ludwig Kirchner had a black-and-white photo of Cranach's painting in his studio in Berlin, where he settled in 1911 and where he painted the *Nude with Hat*. Kirchner considered Cranach's *Venus* to be ideal in every respect, and with this source of inspiration he dared to refer to the art of an earlier age. Kirchner painted the background expressively, presenting the curtain, table, carafe, and glasses as a complete, unified work of art in itself. In contrast to the background, the nude is relatively flat, with sharp outlines. The emphasized flatness and the decisive, contrasting colors stem from Kirchner's own restoration. After moving to Frauenkirch near Davos in Switzerland in 1917, the artists had the paintings that had been stored in Berlin shipped to him. Some were damaged in the process and needed reworking, which provided Kirchner with the opportunity to change a number of them, as he did in this case. He also backdated the nude, which actually shows his friend Doris Grosse (Dodo), a dancer he knew from his days in Dresden. The painting is directly related to Kirchner's sculpture, *Nude Girl*, ca. 1912/13 (see below).   *GM*

Ernst Ludwig Kirchner
(1880–1938)
Nude Girl, ca. 1912/13
Inv. No. SGP 206
Painted wood, height 63 cm

This sculpture is closely related to Ernst Ludwig Kirchner's painting *Nude with Hat*, painted around 1911

(see previous description) and the woodcut *Nude with Black Hat* from 1912/13. Kirchner himself dated the statue to 1917, which seems improbable given his physical condition at that time. More likely he began working on the figure (the features resemble his wife, Erna Schilling) in Berlin around 1912 in connection with the painting and woodcut. When he later moved to Frauenkirch near Davos, in 1917, the contents of his Berlin studio were sent to him. Many of the works arrived damaged, and he most probably decided to finish this one (hence the date) and to rework others.   *GM*

Ernst Ludwig Kirchner
(1880–1938)
Variété
(English Couple Dancing), 1912/13
Inv. No. 2151
Oil on canvas, 151 x 120 cm

The dance scene that Ernst Ludwig Kirchner repeatedly painted played a major role in Expressionist art. The atmosphere in which the dances took place, the unbridled movements of the bodies in artful gowns and evening attire, reflected a passion for life. The proportions of the bodies and their spatial relationships were analogous to the meaning of the painting. Although Kirchner backdated *Variété* to 1907, it belongs stylistically to his work around 1912/13 and was reworked around 1926, retaining the composition. Kirchner then gave the shapes a firmer outline and largely covered up the former light brushwork. Dr. Carl Hagemann purchased the

painting in that state in 1932, and his heirs donated it to the Städel.

GM

Ernst Ludwig Kirchner
(1880–1938)
Two Women at a Basin
(The Sisters)
Inv. No. 2066 (SM-V)
Oil on canvas, 121 x 91 cm

Ernst Ludwig Kirchner's work, along with the works of other Brücke Group members, including Erich Heckel (1883–1970), Karl Schmidt-Rottluff (1884–1976), Emil Nolde (1867–1956) and Otto Müller (1874–1930), make up the heart of the Städel's collection of classical modern art. Despite the enormous losses sustained in 1937 when the National Socialists confiscated art they regarded as degenerate, the quality of the Städel's collection of Expressionist art has remained high, thanks to Dr. Carl Hagemann, a collector and patron of Kirchner,

and his heirs. In a letter to Dr. Hagemann from March 7, 1931, Kirchner dated this painting to 1913 and named it *The Sisters*. It is probably a painting of the Schilling sisters, one of whom Kirchner later married. Stylistically, this date also makes sense because of the increasing angularity of the geometrically formed figures he was painting around that time.

GM

Karl Schmidt-Rottluff (1884–1976)
Red Tower in the Park, 1910
Inv. No. 2139
Oil on canvas, 76 x 85 cm

The place that is depicted is Dangast, near Oldenburg in Northern Germany, where the artists of the Brücke Group repeatedly spent their summers between 1907 and 1912. The view of bushes, trees, pines, and the tower of a country house are painted with confident, quick brushstrokes. The colors red, blue, and green are applied to the canvas in such a way that the grounding shows through, becoming an element of the pictorial language. They form the opposite pole to the unbroken black outline that lends the view its compact form. This illustrates one of the parallels between the dynamic style of the Brücke Group and the painting of the Fauves, who, through their main representative Henri Mattise (1869–1954), were on view at an exhibition organized in Berlin in 1908 by Paul Cassirer.   *GM*

Karl Schmidt-Rottluff (1884–1976)
The Worshipper, 1917/18
Inv. No. St.P 417
Painted wood, height 38 cm

Karl Schmidt-Rottluff tried to find a way of expressing the power of primitive art in his paintings and sculpture, much as did the Fauves, the Cubists and his Expressionist colleagues Ernst Ludwig Kirchner (1880–1938) and Emil Nolde (1867–1956). Following the example set by Pablo Picasso (1881–1973) and Paul Gaugin (1848–1903), they believed to have found this power in the art of the South Seas and Africa. Schmidt-Rottluff collected the art of these cultures and used his collection as a

basis to work from memory while he was stationed in Russia during the World War I. There he carved *The Worshipper* out of wood, later applying lapis lazuli blue pigment to the body and limbs and bronze to the base. Here Schmidt-Rottluff succeeded in creating a representation of the ceremonial act of worship that would be understandable across broad cultural borders.   *GM*

Paula Modersohn-Becker
(1876–1907)
Girl's Head, ca. 1905
Inv. No. SG 1138
Oil on canvas, 25 x 21 cm

Paula Modersohn-Becker saw the work of Paul Gaugin (1848–1903) in Paris in 1905, and was inspired by the way he depicted his subjects. Modersohn-Becker sought her models among the peasants and painted them with natural distance and reserve, contrary to the predominant tendency at the time to portray rural life in a romantic light. Her great talent allowed her to adapt contemporary French painting, and she was

one of the first artists of her period to acknowledge the emergence of modern art.   *GM*

Erich Heckel (1883–1970)
Landscape in Holstein, 1913
Inv. No. SG 1128
Oil on canvas, 82 x 96 cm

This painting is one of the works confiscated by the National Socialists in 1937 that the Städel managed to buy back. It was first listed as Inv. No. SG 403 and was purchased for the Städel's Städische Galerie in 1926 from the Pauline Kowarzik

collection. After it was confiscated it landed in a warehouse in Nieder-schönhausen and was then sold to Bernhard Böhmer in the town of Güstrow. Later it was traded for a nother work and eventually found its way into the collection of Karl Buch-holz in Berlin, from whom the Städel bought it back in 1951. The painting, showing the landscape of Flensburg Fjord, where Erich Heckel spent his summers from 1913 to 1943, is among the best of the pictures he painted there. With his powerful style the artist sketched the wind-swept landscape but gave it firm outlines. The quickly shifting cloud formations are painted in an easy, detached style full of contrasting colors and shapes.   *GM*

Wilhelm Lehmbruck (1881–1919)
Sitting Youth (Bowed Figure,
The Friend, The Thinker,
 The Hermit, Tired Warrior) 1916/17
Inv. No. SGP 28
Artificial stone casting,
height 104 cm

This is Wilhelm Lehmbruck's last large sculpture. The inscription in one of his sketches from 1916/17 shows that it was designed to be a war memorial entitled *Tired Warrior.* He began working on the monu-ment in 1916 in Berlin and finished it in 1917, the year he was released from the military, in his new home in Zurich. In addition to a 1918 bronze casting that originally stood in the Duisburg war cemetery (now in the Wilhelm Lehmbruck Museum in Duisburg), there was another artifi-cial stone casting that was donated to the Städtische Kunsthalle in Mannheim from the Sally Falk collection. This was confiscated by the National Socialists in 1937 as de-generate art and later acquired by the National Gallery of Art in Wash-ington, D.C.   *GM*

Franz Marc (1880–1916)
Dog Lying in the Snow,
ca. 1910/11
Inv. No. 2085 (SM-V)
Oil on canvas, 63 x 105 cm

Originally listed as Inv. No. SG 292, this painting was condemned as degenerate art and confiscated from the Städel in 1937. It was bought, presumably by Le Ray W. Berdeau of Florida at the Fischer auction in Lucerne in 1939. The Galerie Beyeler bought it from the collection in 1960 and one year later it was re-purchased by the Friends of the Städel Museum. The date is based on an oil sketch of the same subject dated 1910/11. The painting shows Marc's Siberian Shepherd, Russi, lying in the snow. *GM*

the latter outlined in his 1910 manuscript, "About the Spirituality of Art." In the years from 1925 to 1933 Jawlensky produced the series of portraits called *Constructivist Heads*, which were extremely limited in their subject and form. In his search for the prototype of the portrait he turned to the tradition of the icon, especially the Vera Icon and portrayals of Christ. He restricted himself to a type of face that he painted in a small format in various

Alexei Jawlensky (1864–1941)
Symphony in Pink, 1929
Inv. No. 1855
Oil on canvas mounted on
cardboard, 36 x 27 cm

Alexei Jawlensky developed his approach to painting—the serial treatment of very few picture genres—against the background of Russian Revolutionary art and Wassily Kandinsky's (1866–1944) ideas, which

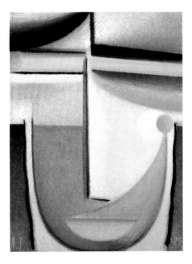

colors. In his correspondence with Benedictine Father Willibrord Verkade he wrote that his meditative "faces" expressed a state of religious emotion. *GM*

Lyonel Feininger (1871–1956)
The Village Pond of Gelmeroda, 1922
Inv. No. 2109 (SM-V)
Oil on canvas, 86 x 112 cm

In countless preparatory studies and paintings for *The Village Pond of Gelmeroda*, Lyonel Feininger addressed the phenomenon of reflections in water. The painting is based on a drawing he called *Notes on Nature*, dated May 20, 1913. The composition of the village, fragmented through color and form, shows how the Cubists and the Futurists influenced Feininger's work, including his musical compositions. It forms the basis of a series of paintings on this subject. *GM*

Paul Klee (1879–1940)
View of the Fertile Land on the Banks of the Nile, 189 (T9), 1932
Inv. No. SG 1221
Oil on cardboard, 49 x 35 cm

The source of inspiration for this painting was Paul Klee's month-long journey to North Africa, which he undertook in December 1928

and which lead him to Egypt. The settled appearance of the architecture and fields along the banks of the Nile impressed him. He condensed what he saw into a rhythmic pictorial structure made up of a variety of lines and points. A unified palette finally lead him to this self-contained landscape composition, which he mentioned in a letter to his wife Lily, explaining that it was the view from the Valley of the Kings into the fertile land on the riverbank. *GM*

Max Ernst (1891–1976)
Aquis Submersus, 1919
Inv. No. SG 1244
Oil on canvas, 54 x 44 cm

Aquis Submersus was among the first Surrealist paintings by Max Ernst, influenced by the *Pittura metafisica* of Giorgio de Chirico (1888–1978) and Carlo Carrà (1881–1966), whose works Ernst saw in reproduction in 1919. Common to the works of the three artists is a sober enumeration of cool-

ly represented facts, which resemble perceived reality but in their decisive elements fade into a dream world. The observer is presented with a narrative already in progress. The beginning is deliberately left unclear, and all that remains are the feelings and premonitions of a reality that perhaps originated in dreams. The reference to the interpretation of dreams is evidence of Ernst's interest in the work of Sigmund Freud. The title of the painting is also the title of a novella by Theodor Storm (1817–1888), which tells the story of forbidden love. In the book the child of the union is abandoned and ultimately dies as a result of its father's negligence. Early critics of this work did not address the psychological but rather the political symbolism, in the context of which the child is seen as a symbol for Germany's failed socialist republic. *GM*

Otto Dix (1891–1969)
The Artist's Family, 1927
Inv. No. 2065 (SM-V)
Oil on wood, 80 x 50 cm

In addition to his famous socio-critical works and his anti-war art, Otto Dix chose subjects borrowed from Early Netherlandish painting, and this portrait of his family derives from the traditional paintings the Holy Family. He painted it following the birth of his son Ursus in Dresden, where he worked as a professor at the Art Academy. Even in this family portrait he departs from the constraints of realism in favor of the style preferred by the "Neue Sachlichkeit" movement. True to form,

he grotesquely exaggerated the physical characteristics of his subjects in order to illustrate their relationship to one another.   *GM*

Pablo Picasso (1881–1973)
Woman's Head (Tête de femme), 1931
Inv. No. St.P 393 (SM-V)
Bronze, 86 x 32 x 49 cm

After a creative phase influenced by Surrealism, Picasso focused on sculpture around 1930, and at that time the model for *Head of a Woman* was created. The sculpture is one of four larger than life-size heads from Pablo Picasso's Boisgeloup period. In producing this series Picasso was most probably influenced by the *Jeannette Heads* that Henri Matisse (1869–1954) created in 1913. Picasso concentrated on volume without structuring the woman's skin. The surface is

basically smooth, with several light, uneven patches. The volume consists of organic bulges and balls that Picasso had already experimented with in sketches from 1907. The phallic nose in the *Woman's Head* has its origin in non-European masks illustrated in the *Cahiers d'Art* and was probably modeled on an 8th-century Japanese Gigaku mask. The autonomous shape of Picasso's sculpture, however, allows it to be viewed from all sides, each view offering its own legitimate sculptural experience. After completing an original in plaster and in wood, Picasso produced an interim model made of plaster, followed by a bronze original, two bronze castings with slightly different bases for the neck (one of which is this *Woman's Head*), as well as a cement casting which Spain exhibited in 1937 at the World Exhibition in Paris.   *GM*

Max Beckmann (1884–1950)
Still Life with Saxophones, 1926
Inv. No. SG 1159
Oil on canvas, 85 x 195 cm

The *Still Life with Saxophones* is among the principle works that Max Beckmann produced during his Frankfurt period. He composed it in an unusual format which emphasizes the dense and tension-filled arrangement. In front of a background consisting of a table and a chair standing in a room begins the independent life of two saxophones, candlesticks, clarinets, sheet music, and other objects whose meaning, with a few exceptions, remains unknown. From a few clues we can reconstruct the world this still life represents. The inscription on one of the saxophones commemorates, for example, a former Frankfurt jazz bar and indicates Beckmann's taste in music. The lettering on the right, (EXHIBITI) ON NEW YORK, could indicate Beckmann's first exhibition, at the I.B. Neumann gallery in New York in 1926. Shortly after it was painted, Städel Director Georg Swarzenski bought it for the Städtische Galerie (Inv. No. SG 436) with help of funds from the Frankfurt

Kunstlerhilfe (artists' aid). It was one of the first of the 77 paintings to be confiscated from the Städel and was removed in 1936 to the warehouse in Niederschönhausen. In 1939 Karl Buchholz purchased the painting for the Kunstmuseum in Basle. Later, however, the sales contract was annulled and the Swiss seller demanded its return in 1940. The Städtische Galerie succeeded in buying the painting back from a Düsseldorf collector. *GM*

Max Beckmann (1884–1950)
Backstage, 1950
Inv. No. SG 1268
Oil on canvas, 102 x 127 cm

The first preparatory sketch for this painting is dated November 1950, and the painting itself was almost finished one day before Max Beckmann's death. A few spots on the trunks of the pine trees still show signs of the pastel that he planned to paint in oil the next day. As is the case with each of Beckmann's works, the meaning of *Backstage* remains enigmatic. The artist referred to the painting in his diary as *Theater Dressing Room* (November 25,

1950), and in another reference he calls it Theater Prop Room (December 19, 1950) and Theater Costumes (December 20/22/26, 1950). A hold of a ship, similar to the one in which he traveled from his exile in Amsterdam to America, bears an arrangement of props from various Beckmann paintings whose reality and alienation are called into question for one last time. *GM*

a perspective laden with emotion and significance. The neutral title of Grand Duc is expressed in unusual materials—here, with oil paint mixed with plaster and, in other pictures in the series, with oil paint mixed with tar. Dubuffet's freedom from the restraints of academic art and his use of materials previously thought to be unworthy of art made him the foremost model for German painters of the postwar period. *GM*

Jean Dubuffet (1901–1985)
Tapié—Grand Duc, August, 1946
Inv. No. SG 1252
Mixed media, 81 x 65 cm

In the same year that Jean Dubuffet began to assemble his collection of Art Brut, he painted this portrait of his friend, the art critic Michel Tapié. It is one of the first of his series of portrait heads from 1946/47 that he called "Plus beaux qu'ils croient" (more beautiful than they believe). Inspired by the art of the mentally disturbed, Dubuffet reduced the features to a minimum of strokes in

Alexander Calder (1898–1976)
Mobile (Red Lily), 1950
Inv. No. St.P 380 (SM-V)
Iron and wire, colored,
height 267 cm

Since 1932 Alexander Calder had
been creating hanging, movable objects that Marcel Duchamp
(1887–1968), who first experimented
with kinetic art around 1925, would
later call "mobiles." Calder's first
mobiles were set in motion by mo-
tors or small manual wind-up de-
vices. Later he used air currents,
sometimes generated by the motion
of the observers. All of this created
what appeared to be random movements of the carefully balanced elements of the mobiles.   *GM*

Alberto Giacometti (1901–1966)
Grand nu assis, 1957
Inv. No. SG 1261
Oil on canvas, 154 x 59 cm

Alberto Giacometti had already exhibited a tendency toward abstract,
non-objective painting in the 1930s,
when he changed his approach to

the representation of human figures. Influenced by Sardinian art and the work of Hermann Haller (1880–1950), he developed a form of expression in which the figure appears in spatial isolation and is shown in minimal physical terms. His work gained popularity when Jean Paul Sartre (1905–1980) interpreted it. Our collection contains the painting for which Giacometti's wife Annette probably modeled. It is part of a group of works that also includes his sculpture *Woman with Broken Shoulder* (Femme, épaule cassée) from 1958/59 and work on paper from the years 1950 to 1965.   *GM*

Eduardo Chillida (born 1924)
Anvil of Dreams VII
(Yunque de sueños VII), 1954/59
Inv. No. SGP 203
Wrought iron on a wooden base,
94 x 48 x 36 cm

Eduardo Chillida's sculptures are based on a tradition started by Julio Gonzales (1876–1942) in 1908, when he made a sculpture of iron and steel because he lacked the money for other materials. Conventional sculpting techniques of modeling clay, chiseling stone, or carving wood had given way to welding, especially in the 1950s and 1960s. This innovation was comparable to paintings of Jean Dubuffet (1901–1985) in that it also used new materials, previously considered unsuitable for art. Chillida, however, incorporated various techniques in his work. In addition to the *Anvil of Dreams* in the Städel, Chillida produced a total of 18 sculptures bearing the same title between 1954 and 1973. These are

composed of the combinations of iron with wood or iron with stone and differ mainly in the melodic sounds they make when worked on the anvil.   *GM*

Francis Bacon (1909–1992)
Study for the Nurse in the Film
Battleship Potemkin, 1957
Inv. No. SG 1248
Oil on canvas, 198 x 142 cm

In 1925 Russian director Sergey Eisenstein (1898–1948) was shooting a film based on the mutiny aboard the battleship Potemkin and the way the military and the population of Odessa reacted to it. One scene in the film, depicting a screaming nurse, particularly interested Francis Bacon and inspired him to create this painting. In it, the woman's huge

mouth, open in terror, and her glasses, shattered by bullets, are still recognizable from the film, although everything else in the scene has been changed completely. Bacon transferred the emphasis from the isolation of the nurse in the film, who emerges from an indifferent throng of people, to the bruised, exposed creature here, trapped in a hopeless, unstable space with no way out.   *GM*

Georg Baselitz
(Hans Georg Kern, born 1938)
Head, 1963
Inv. No. SG 1267
Oil on canvas, 100 x 64

Georg Baselitz's provocative works from the 1960s mark the iconoclastic phase in which he rejected pleasant forms and wrestled with figurative subjects in order to distance himself from the figurative art of National Socialism and Socialist Realism. In 1962 Baselitz and Eugen Schönebeck (*b.* 1936) created *Pan-*

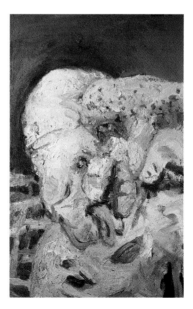

demonium I, based on the works of the Comte de Lautréamont (1847–1870) and Antonin Artaud (1896–1948), and, a year later, *Pandemonium II*. These works presented the viewer with a fermenting substance from which new bodies or body parts were supposed to be created. With his innovations Baselitz consciously stretched the borders of contemporary social tolerance, which lead to the confiscation of two of his works from an exhibition in Berlin in 1963. *GM*

Karel Appel (born 1921)
Portrait of Emmanuel Lootens, 1956
Inv. No. SG 1262
Oil on canvas, 146 x 141 cm

Emmanuel Looten, whom Karel Appel met through art critic Michel Tapié, was the poet/chronicler of Flanders' Celtic history. Appel captured his fiery personality and vitality in the portrait that depicts his features in animalistic exaggeration. Appel, who was one of the founders of the group of artists called COBRA, painted a series of por-

traits that he called *Tête d'orange* in 1955/56. With his gestural painting, focused on the figure, he countered the popular dominant tendency at the time towards non-objective Art Informel. *GM*

Emil Schumacher (born 1912)
Untitled, 1960
Inv. No. 2152 (SM-V)
Oil on canvas, 101 x 81 cm

Emil Schumacher's answer to the geometric abstraction of the 1950s was a style of painting inspired by Art Informel that reduced shapes and contrasts to a minimum and aimed to reveal the process of the paintings creation. Schumacher was primarily interested in the encounter with paint as a medium, and this as well as his stylistic approach described above is evident in his untitled painting from 1960. Here the paint is fissured, enlivened by amorphous signs, and thus transformed into a field of color. Schumacher also used materials previously considered unsuitable for art, such as sand. This shows the

enormous influence of Jean Dubuffet (1901–1985), who demonstrated through Art Brut that entirely new ways of using materials was possible, ending the long search for original art from primitive societies. *GM*

Ernst Wilhelm Nay (1902–1969)
Red Sound
Inv. No. 2095 (SM-V)
Oil on canvas, 240 x 190 cm

Following reconstruction of its building destroyed during World War II and the first re-purchases of art confiscated from its collection, the Städel was able to concentrate on expanding its collection of 20th-century art. The purchase of Ernst Wilhelm Nay's large works marks this new beginning. *Red Sound*, along with *Positive Blue* and *Toledo Yellow* are among the most important "disk" paintings that Nay created between 1954 and 1962. Like so many artists of his generation, Nay

felt liberated by Modernism art of France and the Abstract Expressionism of America. In Germany, the tendency towards gestural painting gave way to the color-field painting of the 1950s and 1960s, which in its use of color was strongly influenced by Nay. *GM*

A. R. Penck
(Ralf Winkler, born 1939)
Small View of the World, Psychotronic-Strategic Art, 1966/71
Inv. No. SG 1264
Oil on canvas, 30 x 40 cm

The 1966 painting, *Small View of the World*, with its clearly recognizable symbols, was the basis for one of the collective actions by artists of the Lücke Group in Dresden: Harald Gallasch (*b.* 1949), Wolfgang Opitz (*b.* 1944), and A.R. Penck. In Penck's "world," human beings in an almond-shaped structure floating around in outer space, continually

experience family, war, and peace. In the action which took place in 1971 in Dresden, Gallasch painted two red heads on Penck's allegory of life. Their subtle communication functions by way of sight and speech. Opitz then pasted five German-Russian Friendship stamps over the eye of the red head shown in profile. These stamps were mandatory "payment" artists had to make in order to be allowed to paint and exhibit in Dresden's Pushkin House. In the final act of this action, Penck painted black stripes through the two heads. *GM*

Gerhard Richter (born 1932)
Large Curtain (163/1), 1967
Inv. No. SG 1274
Oil on canvas, 200 x 280 cm

This painting, exhibited in the 1972 Biennale, was inspired by a floor-length curtain in the Galerie Schmela. It is an illusionistic work which developed from Gerhard Richter's

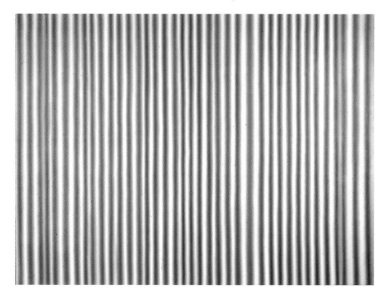

earlier pieces *Morandi* (1964) and *Curtain* (1965/66). The apparent softness of the material takes on a life of its own—the fluency of the folds is emphasized by the cropping of the picture and evokes the work of Fernand Léger (1881–1955). It looks like a large sheet of corrugated iron, which is in fact how the artist referred to it in a notation on the back of the canvas.   *GM*

Sigmar Polke (born in 1941)
Positive Water Drops, 1983
Inv. No. SG 1259
Enamel and acrylic paint on
pre-printed fabric, 180 x 150 cm

Following his apprenticeship as a glass painter, Sigmar Polke studied art under Gerhard Hoehme and Karl Otto Götz at the Düsseldorf Art Academy. There he founded the genre Capitalist Realism in 1963, along with artists Konrad Fischer-Lueg and Gerhard Richter. The group's radical ideas resulted in their first point and halftone paintings and paintings on furnishing fabrics. In the 1980s Polke experimented with

enamel paints, borrowing from techniques he learned as a glass painter, and combined these with his experience in double-exposure photography to create such dazzling works as *Positive Water Drops.*   *GM*

Bernhard Heisig (born 1925)
When the Great Trumpeter Died,
1981/85
Inv. No. 2153 (SM-V)
Oil on canvas, 180 x 135 cm

This expressive composition, originally entitled *Night of the Dead Stars*, was strongly influenced by Max Beckmann (1884–1950). The background consists of a large metropolis at night in an infinite universe. In the foreground stands a tower made of trumpets and symbols identified with the stars of the music world: flowers, applauding hands, open mouths, listening ears. This world is presented to the observer through the television, shown imploded at the top of the tower. Bernhard Heisig changed the title in 1986, dedicating the painting to the memory of Louis Armstrong and his jazz music.   *GM*

Piero Manzoni (1933–1963)
Achrome (Large Seams), 1960
Inv. No. SG 1242
Oil on canvas, 80 x 100 cm

Piero Manzoni created the first of his series *Achromes* after he saw Yves Klein's (1928–1962) monochrome blue paintings in Milan in 1957. From that time until his death in 1963, Manzoni dedicated himself to painting monochrome, seamed canvases. Unlike the works of Yves Klein, Manzoni's paintings refer only to themselves and represent in their two-dimensionality nothing more than the means and technique of pure painting. Along with Lucio Fontana (*b*. 1933), Manzoni joined the Gruppo Nucleare in 1957. Later he became a member of the Group Zero. Along with fellow artists Heinz Mack (*b*. 1931) and Otto Piene (*b*. 1928) he signed the Zero Manifesto—against nothing. His works are a radical rejection of the meaning of what is represented and proclaim the essential material existence of art. *GM*

Yves Klein (1928–1962)
Blue Sponge Relief
(Kleine Nachtmusik), 1960
Inv. No. SG 1254
Sponge, stone, and pigments
on wood and canvas,
145 x 116 cm

This work, which was originally with Georges Marci de Saqquarah in Gstaad and later Nikolaus Bourard in Zurich, is part of a series of paintings called Sponge Reliefs, made between 1957 and 1961. In these works Yves Klein combined natural products from the sea with his preferred color, the patented International Klein Blue. The items are not set into the picture but are altered and painted over to become aesthetic objects. In 1960 Klein founded the Nouveau Réalisme group along with Pierre Restany (*b*. 1930). Its goal was to combat the influence of the Tachism style of painting, dominant at the time and to set themselves against American Pop Art and its imitation of reality. The subtitle, *Kleine Nachtmusik*, is a play on

the artist's name Klein and refers to the music he played while creating this work. *GM*

Antoni Tàpies (born 1923)
Great White with Bedframe
(Grand blanc à la cage), 1965
Inv. No. SG 1253
Mixed media on canvas mounted on wood, 195 x 130 cm

Antoni Tàpies exhibited with Jean Dubuffet (1901–1985) in 1957 in Barcelona. For Tàpies, Dubuffet's Art Brut signified that his own art, which is rooted in Surrealism, could be experienced through the senses. Not only optical phenomena but also tactile materials serve the chain of associations inherent in a painting. For *Great White with Bedframe*, Tàpies used a grainy mixture made up of paint, sand, and marble dust held together by glue to create a surface relief protruding into the foreground. Tàpies' humanistic, existen-

tial philosophy, based primarily on the works of Marcel Duchamp (1887–1968), lead him to a formal reference to Albrecht Dürer's monogram, which appears in the painting as embroidery on the white bed linen. *GM*

Blinky Palermo (1943–1977)
Untitled (Fabric Painting), 1970
Inv. No. SG 1263
Dyed linen woven with cotton and backed by natural colored nettle, 200 x 70 cm

Blinky Palermo radicalized the work begun by Jean Dubuffet (1901–1985) and Marcel Duchamp (1887–1968) in that he reduced the artistic act to choosing the available materials and determining the size and proportion of the work. In 1967 he created his first horizontal pieces made out of upholstery that he had sewn together. Their colors, similar to painted ones, developed their own individual energies. The natural consequence of this was an association with landscape painting, which he tried to avoid with the extreme vertical format, which creates the predominant impression. Ulrich Rückriem's 1984 sculpture *Split Granite* (see below) illustrates the powerful influence Palermo's work had on artists of the 1970s and 1980s. *GM*

Ulrich Rückriem (born 1938)
Split Granite, 1984
Inv. No. SGP 215
Light gray Finnish granite, 10 x 1.2 x 1.5 m

As the apex of an imaginary isosceles triangle covering the grounds of the Städel, the base of which was defined by two monumental stones on the lawn of the Städel garden, the granite stele on the shore of the River Main was the focal point of an Ulrich Rückriem exhibition at the Städtische Galerie from 1984 to 1986. For the sculpture overlooking the river, Rückriem chose a slab of granite that was split into five parts. By turning the split granite 180 degrees, about 150 centimeters of it was sunk into the ground as its base, while approximately 850 centimeters remained visible. Rückriem chose the dimensions, location, and color of the stele with respect to the course of the central axis of the entrance to the Städel and the skyline of Frankfurt's bank towers on the opposite side of the river.   *GM*

Anselm Kiefer (born 1945)
The Conquests of Alexander
the Great, 1987/88
Inv. No. SG 1269
Chalk, photo, and prepared lead
Label on the surface: "Saturn Lead".
350 x 640 cm

This work, in the form of a classical historic painting, evolved in Anselm Kiefer's former studio in Buchen in Odenwald. The lead lay flat on the floor of his work space and initially served as a projection surface. It was soon marked by traces of both planned and accidental activity. When it was finally raised and mounted on a wooden scaffold it showed lighter colored "islands" and dark "canals." When the artist applied chalk drawings it developed into a sort of map. Then he added details taken from the history of Alexander the Great, the Macedonian king whose army advanced to the heart of the Persian Empire in the 3rd century B.C. The initial associations give way to knowledge at this point. On an attached sheet of lead Kiefer drew a chalk knot with the inscription "Gordon." Just as he should read "Gordian", the observer makes mistakes in remembering history lessons about the conquests of Alexander's army, so that only a vague notion of great distances, armies, and impossible tasks remain. Although purchased earlier, this work, along with *Palette with Wings*

(see below), was part of a Kiefer installation entitled *About Space and People*, shown at the Städel in 1990.   GM

Anselm Kiefer (born 1945)
Palette with Wings, 1985
Inv. No. SGP 219
Lead, steel, and tin
2.5 x 7 x 1.4 m

The palette was a subject in Anselm Keifer's paintings as early as the 1970s. The first winged palette appeared in *Resumptio*, a painting he made in 1974. Eleven years later he used it again as the subject of his first lead sculpture. A smaller version followed that, along with lead books, shelves, and airplanes. The spread wings are reminiscent of the representations of Nike from the 19th century, particularly those on the Schlossbrücke in Berlin, which Kiefer used in his book *Symboles Héroïques*. With this he indicated that the wing motif is a symbol of the healing power of art. But here the heavy weight of the lead wings and their damaged edges seem to indicate the exact opposite. Following the opening of the Städel's new annex in 1990, the *Palette with Wings* was part of Kiefer's installation *About Space and People* (compare to previous work). The *Palette* now graces the Städel Café.   GM

Dan Flavin (1933–1996)
Untitled
(for Professor Klaus Gallwitz),
1993
Inv. No. SGP 220
Installation made up of 132 fluorescent light fixtures in pink, blue, red, ultraviolet, green, and yellow, each 120 cm long

Dan Flavin conceived this installation for an exhibition entitled *Light Rooms: Inside and Outside*, which took place in 1993 in both ground-floor rooms of the new annex to the Städel. Beginning in 1993 Flavin had

rows, in geometrical groups, or by color. Their placement was determined by the spatial conditions of the room in which they were installed. For the Städel's new annex, Flavin chose the columns whose distance to the wall (or to the next column) he bridged with three parallel rows of light fixtures. In doing so he cast a cool blue light over the smaller of the two exhibition rooms, while in the larger room pink, yellow, blue, and green lights connected the corresponding pairs of columns. As a result, each visitor that passes through the room casts a four-color shadow on the wall opposite the lights. *GM*

been creating works using industrial fluorescent light fixtures in the tradition of Minimal Art. He varied the works by arranging the fixtures in

The Department of Prints and Drawings

The Department of Prints and Drawings of the Städel Art Institute is located in the left wing of the main building. Although it attracts less attention from most of the visitors than the Painting Gallery does, it is one of the most significant collections in Germany, and art historians from Germany and abroad are as familiar with it as they are with the Painting Gallery. Similar to the Painting Gallery, the Print Collection is strongly determined by the Institute's history, which begins with its founding in the late 18th century and continues its versatile development into the present.

The collection covers 600 years of history of the graphic arts and contains examples from all of Europe's most important schools. About one-third of the circa 100,000

sheets are drawings, and two-thirds are prints. The collection owes its foundation around 1800 to two Frankfurt citizens, banker Johann Friedrich Städel and his friend, attorney Dr. Johann Georg Grambs. Both of these men were impressed by the educational value of understanding art within its full context. They regarded art not only as something to be enjoyed by the informed observer but simultaneously as an effective medium for the acquisition of knowledge.

In the 19th century Johann David Passavant gave the collection the structure it has today. As inspector (the original title of his position) he ran the institute from 1840 to 1861. Passavant, who started as a painter and a friend of the Nazarenes and who later became foremost a histo-

Antonio Pollaiuolo (1431/32–1498), The Battle of the Gladiators, ca. 1470/75, Inv. No. 34115, Engraving, 410 x 600 mm, Gift of Johann David Passavant before 1862

rian, was considered to be one of Europe's leading art experts. He was particularly interested in the graphic arts, but despite his specialization he maintained a broad intellectual horizon and had a keen sense for quality, both of which enabled him to acquire spectacular works from many different periods. It was because of Passavant that drawings by Albrecht Dürer, Raphael, Rembrandt, and Jean-Antoine Watteau, among others, found their way into the Frankfurt collection. Passavant also recognized the difference between prints as reproductions, which were to prove useful as a teaching aid at the Städel Art School, and prints as an autonomous form of artistic expression. This early art historian's interests ranged from works by Old Masters to those by his contemporaries. As a result the collection has a wealth of German drawings from the early 19th century in which artists of the Nazarene School are especially well represented.

Georg Swarzenski, who headed the Institute from 1906 until his emigration in 1938, continued Passavant's work in a similar spirit. He resembled Passavant not only in his broad knowledge of art history, but in his receptiveness to the modern art of his time. Both men reflected the museum's role as an institution. Swarzenski's achievement was the foundation of the Städtische Galerie—administered by the Städel Institute—through which the city of Frankfurt could participate along with the Städel foundation in the acquisition of works for this department. This was especially important for the collection of modern and contemporary works. For the first time in the history of the institute, a curator was appointed in 1920 who was solely responsible for the Department of Prints and Drawings.

His name was Edmund Schilling and, together with Georg Swarzenski, he expanded the collection by acquiring Impressionist art as well as German art, with special emphasis on the 16th century, Southern German Rococo and German Romanticism. In this way the Department of Prints and Drawings grew in terms of historical and contemporary art.

The Städel and many other German art institutes suffered under the attacks against modern art by the National Socialists, who condemned many works of art as degenerate. More than 700 works on paper were confiscated, and the loss could never be fully recovered. Nevertheless, the Städel's Department of Prints and Drawings today possesses an excellent range of expressionist art thanks to Dr. Carl Hagemann, who donated his collection with its emphasis on art of the Brücke Group and works by Ernst Ludwig Kirchner. His collection has given the Städel a significant new accent. This also applies to the postwar bequest of the Friedel and Ugi Battenberg collection, which contains a large number of prints by Max Beckmann. A notable contribution also came from the purchase of the Helmut Goedeckemeyer collection, containing the most comprehensive holding of works by Käthe Kollwitz in Germany.

Albrecht Dürer
(1471–1528), Woman from Nuremberg and Woman from Venice, ca. 1495, Inv. No. 696, Pen and ink in brown-black, 245 x 160 mm. Acquired for the Städel by Johann David Passavant before 1862

The next phase of acquisitions concentrated on French art of the 19th century in order to balance out the comprehensive collection of German prints and also because of its significance to the development of modern art. Works by artists such as Théodore Géricault, Eugène Delacroix, Honoré Daumier, and Paul Cézanne were among the new acquisitions. To provide a contrast to the many works of German Expressionists, the Department of Prints and Drawings acquired drawings and prints by Pablo Picasso, Henri Matisse, Alberto Giacometti, and Constructivist artists. Contemporary art included American artists of the 1950s, among them Jackson Pollock, Barnett Newman, Robert Rauschenberg, and Jasper Johns. Special interest was also paid to drawings by sculptors, for example by Eduardo Chillida and Richard Serra.

In addition to serving the needs of art historians, the goal of the curator is to make this collection increasingly available to the general public. The activities focus on the graphic arts as an autonomous field but also correspond and provide orientation to the Painting Gallery. Exhibitions of works from the department's own

Carl Philipp Fohr (1795–1818), Tirolean Landscape with the Ruins of Fragenstein, near Innsbruck, 1815, Inv. No. 226, Pen and ink in gray over pencil with watercolor, 340 x 438 mm. Acquired in 1843 by Johann David Passavant

Paul Cézanne (1839–1906), Allée des Maronniers au "Jas de Bouffan", ca. 1884/87, Inv. No. 16334, Watercolor over pencil, 300 x 470 mm. Acquired in 1976

holdings along with larger presentations on loan with drawings or prints from outside institutions provide visitors with an ever-changing program which always yields something new to be discovered. In 1999 the area occupied by the Department of Prints and Drawings underwent significant structural changes to serve this purpose.

Richard Serra (born 1939), Inca, 1989, Inv. No. SG 1271 (painting catalogue), chalk crayon on paper, 286.5 x 525 cm, Acquired in 1990 for the Städtische Galerie in the Städel Art Institute

Index of Artists

Front cover: Ernst Ludwig Kirchner, *Nude with Hat*, ca. 1911, see p. 126
Back cover: Lucas Cranach the Elder, *Venus*, 1552, see p. 41

Photographic credits:

Artothek:
Inv. Nos. 763, 767, 805, 915, 1015, 1340, 1351, 1370, 1433, 1466, 1476, 1789, 1821, 1987, 2064; SG 170, SG 176, SG 237, SG 264, SG 320, SG 365, SG 404, SG 637, SG 1140, SG 1168, SG 1198, SG 1229
Ursula Edelmann Frankfurt a.M.:
Inv. Nos. 1068, 1109, 1140, 1200, 1221, 1444, 1457, 1498, 1559, 1585, 2158; SG 465, SG 1271; SGP 28, SGP 63, SGP 79b, SGP 195, SGP 203, SGP 206, SGP 215, SGP 219, SGP 220; St.P 373, St.P 374, St.P 380, St.P 389, St.P 393, St.P 416, St.P 417, St.P 439; Graph. Slg. Inv. Nos. 226, 1040, 16069, 16334, 34115; Façade
Kurt Haase, Frankfurt a.M.:
Inv. Nos. 121, 249, 892, 959, 1217, 1436, 1805, 1888; LG BRD (Böcklin); SG 238, SG 640
Jürgen Littkemann, Berlin:
SGP 220

All other photographs of works in the collection are by Jochen Beyer, Village-Neuf.
The architectural photographs are by Horst Ziegenfusz, Frankfurt a.M.

Die Deutsche Bibliothek – CIP-Einheitsaufnahme
Städelsches Kunstinstitut and Städtische Galerie, Frankfurt am Main / Bodo Brinkmann. –
   Munich ; London ; New York : Prestel, 2000
   (Prestel Museum Guide)
   ISBN 3-7913-2169-2

Translated from the German by Mariana Schroeder
Copyedited by Judith Gilbert

Mandlstrasse 26 · 80802 Munich
Tel. (089) 381709-0, Fax (089) 381709-35;
4 Bloomsbury Place · London WC1A 2QA
Tel. (020) 7323 5004, Fax (020) 7636 8004;
175 Fifth Avenue, New York, NY 10010
Tel. (212) 995 27 20, Fax (212) 995 2733

Design and layout by Verlagsservice G. Pfeifer, Germering
Typeset by EDV-Fotosatz Huber, Germering
Lithography by Repro Brüll, Saalfelden
Printed and bound by Passavia Druckservice GmbH., Passau

Printed in Germany on acid-free paper

ISBN 3-7913-2169-2

Prestel Museum Guides

Alte Nationalgalerie
Berlin

3-7913-1733-4

Alte Pinakothek
Munich

3-7913-2239-7

Gemäldegalerie
Berlin

3-7913-1912-4

Hamburger Bahnhof
Berlin

3-7913-1731-8

Hamburger
Kunsthalle

3-7913-1429-7

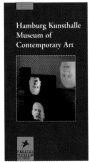

Hamburg Kunsthalle
Museum of
Contemporary Art

3-7913-1899-3

Wilhelm Lehmbruck
Museum
Duisburg

3-7913-2115-3

Lenbachhaus
Munich

3-7913-1623-0

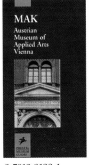

MAK
Austrian
Museum of
Applied Arts
Vienna

3-7913-2133-1

Neue Nationalgalerie
Berlin

3-7913-1732-6

Neue Pinakothek
Munich

3-7913-2240-0

Neues Museum
Nuremberg

3-7913-2318-0

Österreichische
Galerie Belvedere
Vienna

3-7913-1622-2

The Reichstag
Berlin

3-7913-2260-5

The Schloss Moyland
Museum

Van der Grinten Collection

3-7913-1877-2

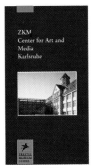

ZKM
Center for Art and
Media
Karlsruhe

3-7913-1883-7